BOARD BOUND Leadership

The Four Essentials

Leadership Governance

Assessment Fundraising

By Dr. Victoria Boyd &
Linda Lysakowski, ACFRE

Galaxy Publishing/Board Bound
848 N. Rainbow #4450
Las Vegas, Nevada 89107
admin@bbleaders.com

Ordering Information Special discounts are available on bulk purchases by corporations, associations, nonprofits, training centers, sales outlets and others. For details, contact the publisher at the address above.
Printed in the United States of America.

Title: Board Bound Leadership: The Four Essentials – Leadership, Governance, Assessment, Fundraising

Boyd, Victoria; Lysakowski, Linda
ISBN 978-0-9854219-1-5 paperback
ISBN 978-0-9854219-2-2 ebook

1. Main category: Personal Growth, Business Management
2. Sub-categories: Nonprofit leadership, governance, assessment, fundraising,

First Edition

About the Authors

Dr. **Victoria Boyd** is founder of The Philantrepreneur Foundation™ and has been a driving force in education and nonprofit arenas as an author, trainer, administrator, and advocate throughout the country. Dr. Boyd recognized early that her passion was to help others and began her career as an educator. Concurrent to teaching Dr. Boyd was active and supportive of many nonprofit organizations serving in numerous leadership capacities such as founder, board member, president, and interim executive director.

Throughout her thirty-two years in the educational arena she was a teacher and state consultant. She experienced extraordinary opportunities and toured with her students throughout the United States and around the globe to places such as England, Scotland, and France. As an educator, she was awarded the *National Educator of the Year* by the National Dance Association, *Educator of the Year* by Michigan and Midwest District of the American Association of Health, Physical Education, Recreation and Dance, the *Golden Apple Award* by Wayne County Regional Educational Service Agency (Wayne RESA), recognized in *Who's Who in America's Teachers*, Wayne State

University's *Arts Achievement Award* and ArtServe Michigan's *Advocate of the Year*. An award that she is most proud to receive was the *Fulbright Memorial Teacher Award* where she studied the educational system in Japan for an extended period.

Since moving to Las Vegas region she shares her expertise as an instructor of Nonprofit Management at UNLV. Her impact continues to be recognized as she has been honored as 2014 Nevada Distinguished Men and Women; 2015 NAWBO Women of Distinction; 2015 LVBMN Entrepreneur Achievement Award, and 2016 and 2017 MyVegas Magazine recognition as a Top 100 Most Influential Women.

The Philantrepreneur Foundation™ (TPF) is a nonprofit *for* nonprofits which builds capacity through education, awareness, and resources. Under TPF's umbrella Dr. Boyd develops resources and training based on the critical needs of the sector.

Dr. Boyd has authored two books,
The Wealthy Teacher: Answering the Question, What's Next? and
WOW 'Em: Webinar Secrets from the Wealthy Teacher.
Co-authored: *How I Did It!*

Linda Lysakowski, ACFRE is one of slightly more than one hundred professionals worldwide to hold the Advanced Certified Fund Raising Executive designation. In her thirty years in the development field, she has managed capital campaigns; helped dozens of nonprofit organizations achieve their development goals, and has trained more than 37,000 professionals in Mexico, Canada, Egypt, Bermuda, and most of the fifty United States. Linda is a graduate of Alvernia University in Reading, PA with majors in Banking and Finance; Communications; and Theology/Philosophy. She is a graduate of AFP's Faculty Training Academy and has received two AFP research grants. She is also a prolific writer, having written or contributed to more than a dozen books. She serves as Acquisitions Editor for CharityChannel Press and For the GENIUS Press. Linda has received the Outstanding Fundraising Executive award from the Eastern PA, Las Vegas, and Sierra (NV) chapters of AFP (Association of Fundraising Professionals) was recognized internationally with the Barbara Marion Award for Outstanding Service to AFP. She was honored with the Lifetime Achievement Award from the Las Vegas Chapter of AFP in November 2015.

Full Length Books

- *Recruiting and Training Fundraising Volunteers*
- *The Development Plan*
- *Fundraising as a Career: What, Are You Crazy?*
- *Capital Campaigns: Everything You NEED to Know*
- *Are You Ready for a Capital Campaign?* workbook
- *Raise More Money from Your Business Community*
- *Raise More Money from Your Business Community—The Workbook*
- *Fundraising for the GENIUS*, 2nd edition
- *Asking Styles 2nd edition*
- *The Leaky Bucket: What's Wrong with Your Fundraising: And How You Can Fix It* (co-author)
- *The Essential Nonprofit Fundraising Handbook* (co-author)
- *Nonprofit Strategic Planning* (co-author)
- *CharityChannel's Quick Guide to Developing Your Case for Support* (co-author)
- *CharityChannel's Quick Guide to Creating a Development Plan* (co-author)
- *The New Donor* (co-author)
- *The Fundraising Feasibility Study* (contributing author)
- *YOU and Your Nonprofit Board* (contributing author)
- *YOU and Your Nonprofit* (co-editor)

- *The Nonprofit Consulting Playbook* (co-editor)
- *The Matriarch* (a novel)

In addition to her full-length books, Linda has written three AFP Ready Reference Books and has been published in numerous other Publications including *International Journal of Nonprofit and Voluntary Sector Marketing, Contributions, Advancing Philanthropy, Associations Now,* CASE *Currents, Major Gifts Report, Grant Station, New Directions in Philanthropy,* and more.

BOARD
BOUND
LEADERSHIP

Authors' Acknowledgements

Special gratitude and acknowledgement to all the individuals from every walk of life that tap into their passion to unselfishly and tireless dedicate energy and time to serve on nonprofit boards of directors. We are here now to serve you.

We'd also like to acknowledge all the boards and executive directors we've worked with over the years for their dedication to the nonprofit sector. And to our fellow consultants to nonprofits, all of whom have worked tirelessly to make the third sector an impactful force, changing the world for the better.

BOARD BOUND LEADERSHIP

$\mathcal{T}$ABLE OF $\mathcal{C}$ONTENTS

About the Authors
Author's Acknowledgements

Foreword   2
Chapter 1   The WHY Factor   5
Chapter 2   Building the Foundation   15
Chapter 3   Busting the Myths   27
Chapter 4   Using the Modules   41
Chapter 5   Module 1: Leadership   45
Chapter 6   Module 2: Governance   55
Chapter 7   Module 3: Assessment   74
Chapter 8   Module 4: Fundraising   90
Chapter 9   Board Bound Ready   114

Appendix   122
The Unique For-Purpose Organization: Startup tips and more….
Quiz Scorecards
Resources

*F*oreword

Ah, the governing board. Of all elements of the nonprofit organization, the governing body – the board of directors, the board of trustees, or whatever you call it – may be the most misunderstood and myth-ridden one, even surpassing confusion around the fundraising function. In North America, all legally registered not-profit-organizations are required by law to seat a governing body of some sort. Beyond that rather vague description, out there in the real world of the vast majority of small nonprofits (that is, those with incomes below $500,000), it's a free for all.

Is the board supposed to govern? What does that mean anyway? Is the board supposed to raise money, and if so how should they do it? Is the board meeting a chance to sit around a table and listen to employees read reports? Is the board's job to run programs, or manage events, or fill in when the Executive Director is too busy? Does the board report to the Executive Director or does the Executive Director report to the board? Of course you may be saying to yourself, we know how to govern, or raise money, or fill in when our ED is too busy. Of course we know who reports to whom. But the question remains, *should* you be doing those things, *when* are they the right things to do, and *have* you and your fellow board members made deliberate, thoughtful decisions about how and when to do them and for what purpose. Oh, and by the way, who does report to whom?

Smaller nonprofits, and many who wish to serve them in some capacity, view the role of the board in so many ways it can be hard to understand what they have in mind, but the four essential elements don't always make it into the list. As Boyd and Lysakowski shows so clearly in this volume, the organization's governing body must, in fact, exercise and balance the four obligations of leadership, governance, assessment, and fundraising. Even better, they show how to meet these obligations as members of the governing body of the organization, rather than acting as adjunct staff or super-volunteers.

Understanding the differing roles of the governing body versus the rest of the organization, and they are significant, has given rise to a great deal of confusion, complexity and uncertainty. In this short, straightforward, workbook-style volume, the authors shine the clear light of day on what it really means to serve on, and act as, a member of the governing body of a nonprofit.

Board Bound Leadership is a great addition to the literature on board service, which ranges from the overly simple to the academic. It's a must-read for small and startup organizations, where confusion about board service tends to be greatest. It's also essential reading for anyone aspiring to serve on a nonprofit board, who is new to board service, or who has board experience but questions whether the board they serve on is really up to standards. As the authors intended, this book takes the mystery out of what it means to join and serve on a board. And it has some great insights on how the nonprofit organization should go about recruiting and preparing individuals to serve on its governing board.

As you read this book, take advantage of the quizzes, assessments, generous spaces for note-taking and suggested reading list. Serving as a member of a nonprofit governing board is an honor, a privilege, and should be a great source of joy - as long as you and the board to which you belong know what you're doing.

I wish to thank the authors for writing this book, and for their generosity in referring to my work on fundraising effectiveness.

Ellen Bristol
Bristol Strategy Group

CHAPTER 1

*7*he Why Factor

French philosophers called it raison d'être — your reason for being.

WHY – a little word that carries so much weight. Therefore we are big promoters of starting with and understanding *why*, before moving on to other areas. Within this book there will be a lot of *why* moments aimed to bring clarity on what it means to be on a nonprofit board of directors.

> Why(h)wi/
> Adverb
> What reason or purpose

We will examine the unique nonprofit world from a board of director's point of view and explore this role because it is one of the most misunderstood and challenging, yet so rewarding. So, starting with why, we will explore,

- The power of why.
- Why we wrote the book and for whom?
- Why it is relevant to the sector?
- Why it is important for you?

So let us begin with the power of why.

In 2009, Simon Sinek introduced a concept which led him to publish a book in 2011, *Start with Why*. In his book, he introduced the *Golden Circle*, a model which flipped the business concept inside out by emphasizing to start with *why* rather than the *what*. Sinek starts with a fundamental question: Why are some people and organizations more innovative, more influential, and more profitable than others? Why do some command greater loyalty from customers and employees alike? Sinek utilizes his powerful *Golden Circle*, to create a framework upon which organizations can build, lead, and inspire people. And it all starts with *why*.

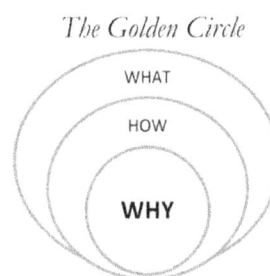

So, what does that have to do with nonprofit board service and leadership?

Everything!

When we started our careers many years ago, of course we hadn't heard of Sinek's *Golden Circle*. It didn't exist. The reality is some careers are magnets for those that follow their *why* naturally. As an educator, Victoria fed her passion for the arts and served her core value to help others reach their full potential. Still to this day her *why* is the compass which helps her gain focus, get motivated to do more, and is the inspiration for the work and path she follows. The nonprofit sector attracts individuals that have a strong passion to serve – that are led by their *why*.

For Linda, starting her career in the business world lent a different perspective. Many times, in the business world and, as Linda found out later, also happens in the nonprofit world, people are focused on the end results and often didn't question the *why*. The day-to-day pressures cause many of us to focus on what we need to do and how to do it.

So why are Victoria, as a former teacher, and Linda, as a former banker, qualified to tackle this topic? We're sure you've heard the many stories of classroom teachers using their own funds to supplement necessary supplies for their classes. Well as a dance teacher it she had additional challenges. School districts don't, well at least Victoria's didn't, provide any funding for dance supplies. So, multiplying the funding need by 100 percent for a dance teacher, she was faced with a funding shortage on the very first day of every school year and it was necessary that she become proficient in fundraising pronto. Victoria was forced to jump in the deep end of the pool before knowing how to swim, introduction by fire, steep learning curve.... we could go on and on with the metaphors. However, it was the best and most valuable stepping stone for Victoria because she went on to become involved with and lead some great nonprofit organizations.

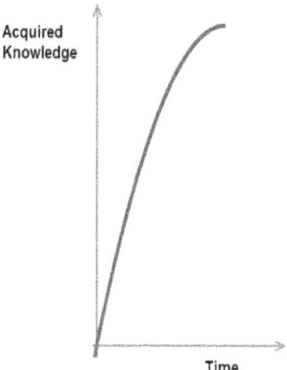

Likewise, Linda worked for nonprofits that were always conscious of how much they were spending, and how much they needed to raise in order to continue to provide needed programs in the community. And we both faced boards that were very conscious of the budget restraints and expected nonprofits to deliver amazing programs serving multiple community needs with very little resources.

What we both recognized early on were the similarities that attracted individuals to both the education and nonprofit sectors - the passion, the values, and the desire to give back - a conscience choice. Our ideals are so powerful we chose our *why* over more lucrative career paths that offer more luxurious perks or benefits. Yes, it is a choice.

Why We Wrote This Book

The Alliance for Nonprofit Management released a 2016 survey called *Voices from Board Chairs* where they surveyed 635 board members and asked what they needed to become effective board members. Their answers led to seven recommendations for nonprofits:

1. Develop a well-planned process of preparation for the board chair and a strong succession plan
2. Clarify the role of the board's relationship to the CEO
3. Provide coaching, training, and mentoring for board chairs
4. Build leadership capacity for committee chairs and other board members
5. Provide research-based resources for board members
6. Support the board chair's leadership function in respect to advocacy and community involvement
7. Move from a heroic form of leadership, where one person is the face and voice of the organization, to a model of shared leadership

These seven recommendations are valid and we take each seriously. We also factored in our over sixty years of combined service to nonprofits, as we heard these themes repeatedly and the question remained for us, who needs board training and why?

We believe this book is a valuable resource for:

- **Existing boards of nonprofit organizations,** which together are committed to enhancing their skills and capabilities to provide effective leadership and governance to their organization and its mission.

- **Individuals** currently on nonprofit boards or aspiring to board membership who want to be more fully prepared to understand

and handle the responsibilities of purposeful board membership, from legal liability to strategic planning.

- **Socially responsible corporations and businesses** that want to develop additional leadership skills in select executives to enable them to fully represent their company as a contributing member of a community organizations leadership team.

Why It Is Relevant To The Sector

So now we've come full circle, using our *why* as the compass to focus on improving nonprofit management, especially board effectiveness. We will help answer questions such as:

- How to improve a board's effectiveness in leadership, governance, assessment, and fundraising?
- How to ensure board members know their job?
- How to know the choices made are best for the organization?
- How to streamline board recruiting and orientation process?

And maybe even a more basic question - what the heck is this board service all about anyway?

These are critical questions that for us after working on the inside and now on the outside we have gained an advantage and unique perspective of its needs and challenges. Think of that aerial view perspective where all the components can be assessed. This view lead to the realization that for boards there are many working parts yet very few, if any, comprehensive programs which identified and clarified the various aspects of their job, and explored the unique attributes of their role that impacts overall success, in the organization and within the sector.

Why It Is Important For You

Board Bound Leadership was born to help answer many of your questions and to help you clearly define your why and the nonprofit organization's why. It will shift nonprofit board membership from being challenging and scary, to a productive, engaging, and

> *"Leaders are the ones who have the courage to go first, to put themselves at personal risk to open a path for others to follow."*
> *Simon Sinek*

valuable experience. It will help define how to make all the members assets versus place holders. More importantly **Board Bound Leadership** identifies the *why* of each board member's role and why they are so vital to current and future success of every nonprofit organization.

Are these your *why*s?

- You want your nonprofit organization to be successful. Well, yeah...
- You want to possess the skills, be confident, and lead with perfection. Removing the fear...
- You want to not just be good but a *great* board member. To be an asset...
- You want to ensure the organization will *thrive* not merely survive? A resounding, "Yes!"

This is *why* everyone involved with a nonprofit organization needs this information. We've moved beyond the era where the cause was enough to sustain a nonprofit. The foundation and key to success is developing an effective and strong board of directors that can lead the organization into the future. Leaders that understand the unique aspects of nonprofit success and can utilize solid business practices to guide a *for-purpose* business.

You'll notice we said *for-purpose* business, not *nonprofit*. We'll talk more about this later but we think the terminology is important and that we need to stop thinking about nonprofits as the stepchildren of society! So, we'd like to change the way you think and talk about the nonprofit sector.

Board Bound Leadership is the opportunity to assess your own understanding of the sector and your preparedness for board service. Assessment is a vital component to heighten awareness of the needs and is essential in the learning process. We use the term *process* just like the choreographic process which involves exploring meaning, learning to communicate through the language of dance, and to create impact for the audience. This process is more important and valuable than the actual performance. The performance is the reward for work well done and executed successfully.

A process is so applicable to the growth and sustainability of a nonprofit organization that it needs to have in place a continuous and ongoing system which includes,
- Leader Adaptability
- Assessing for Impact
- Continuous Improvement

Board Bound Leadership is a system that encourages and rewards a culture of learning.

You Set the Standards

As an individual you might be currently serving on a board or aspiring to serve. Use this book to ensure you are or will be an effective board member. However, there are additional uses we recommend.
- Use it as the benchmark and prerequisite for establishing board qualifications.

- Use it as a group to get the entire board "on board" with becoming more effective at leadership, governance, assessment, and fundraising.
- Even better: we suggest you take the **_Board Bound Leadership_** class as a board and work on the book together.

Whichever method you choose, we are providing a notes page at the end of each chapter so you can capture key ideas and discuss them further. We also provide resources in the appendix for those who want to learn more about various aspects of board service and the about the nonprofit world in general.

So, grab a seat and let's explore the nonprofit sector, your own interest and capabilities, and together build strong nonprofit organizations across the country.

CHAPTER 2

BUILDING THE FOUNDATION

So, why is service on a nonprofit board challenging? Why is it important? Why the nonprofit sector is sometimes called the third sector, and how is it different and unique among other sectors (business, government)?

Oh, let us count the ways…

Why It Was Formed

Organizations for public benefit can be traced back to the 1800s; however the Revenue Act of 1954, sometimes called the Johnson Act, is referenced as the origin of the modern-day tax code which includes section 501(c) for exempt organizations. Over the years, and we won't bore you with the details, the tax code has undergone various legislative adjustments adding or removing requirements. To some, nonprofit organizations remain a mystery surrounded by the unique attributes of leadership, governance, assessment, and that almighty area of fundraising that is guided by legal regulations, program stipulations, a foundation of volunteerism, and the dual message to who you serve and who supports you. The elements related to leadership, governance, assessment, and fundraising is where understanding of the sector and applying unique best practices, principles and strategies for organizational and program success is vital. The entrepreneurial mindset is great to have but it must be combined with philanthropic systems. It's no surprise that some accountants and lawyers steer clear of all things nonprofit.

Don't Settle

So, what can you do? We must take it upon ourselves to educate, bring awareness, and find the resources we need so the nonprofits we serve will be well informed, effective, and efficient. This is *why* the **Board Bound Leadership** platform is so important for those involved in the sector. It will help individuals and board understand the unique aspects, to apply unique nonprofit best practices, and to stay up to date on the ever-changing environment they serve. So, let's explore some of the unique areas that impact the sector.

One unique attribute of nonprofit boards is that there are no specific mandatory qualifications, pre-requisites or skills sets needed to become a member of a board. From every walk of life, individuals are recruited and can join boards by demonstrating a willingness to serve. It's the nature of being a nonprofit with community representation. This brings great diversity but also often comes with questions and statements like, "What is my role?" That's not my job!" or even "I don't know how." It also means that board members aren't guaranteed to have experience or understanding of business practices. Remember this is a nonprofit corporation and must be run as a *for-purpose* business. All of this means it becomes the responsibility of the organization, along with everything else they have to do, to make sure their board is equipped with the skill sets and understanding of board roles and responsibilities. If this is not done, organizations face mediocre performance from their boards. **They settle.**

The board of directors is the axle that turns the organizational wheel. It essentially carries the weight of the organization and it is charged with guiding the vision and ensuring success. This is not fulfilled by just attending meetings but accepting and being a proactive participant fulfilling responsibilities and understanding your role. This level of engagement is vital and considering the points made previously plus the abundance of poverty mindsets, misunderstand the concept of a for-purpose business, or just lack background or experience, is it a challenge? *Yes*. Can it be solved? *Absolutely*!

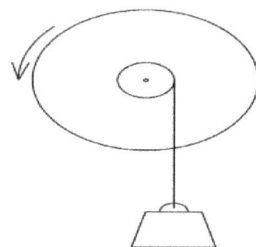

In the nonprofit sector there are no mandated educational requirements, test, boards, or certifications required to be employed in any position. Over the years, universities have added certification programs and nonprofit management degrees, including a PhD in Philanthropy and Development, and several associations such as CFRE International and Association for Fundraising Professionals that created certification programs in their specific area, i.e. the Certified Fund Raising Executive (CFRE International), and the Advanced Certified Fundraising Executive (AFP) designation. However, it remains up to the individual organizations to set job description qualifications. Some of those qualifications are based on a completely different set of competencies such as marketing, finance, or program related skill sets. All good to set a baseline standard but the missing component remains competency in nonprofit management. It is important for you, as a board member, to be aware of these programs when the organization is hiring staff so you can choose people who are serious about their work in the nonprofit sector.

What This All Means for You, as a Board Member

Let us ask you, as a board member, a few questions. How valuable would it be if:

- You and other current or future board members understood their roles and responsibilities?
- That as a board member, you could ensure the sustainability of the organization?
- That each member could be vetted for their capabilities.

In addition, how useful would a toolkit full of documents and resources where leadership, governance, assessment, and fundraising is the focus?

That is the *why* for this book, to fill a gap that is evident in a lack of mandated educational requirements, certifications, and tests to measure a board member's level of expertise.

Unique Leadership

In addition to the unique legal and operational aspects of a nonprofit organization, the roles and responsibilities of its governing body – the board of directors must possess a unique leadership mindset, capabilities,

> **3 Unique Elements**
> - *Motivate without financial incentives*
> - *Non-financial measures of success*
> - *Unifying diverse stakeholders*

and knowledge of those areas to best serve the organization. Wouldn't it be great to have the ability to vet, empower, and ensure that all board members are fully equipped to be an asset to every organization? That the unique nuances of the nonprofit sector are understood and potential candidates know how to use them in practical application. There are certifications for fundraising and general nonprofit management; however, for the board, that is considered the core or axle of the organization, there are very few training options and none that has focused on that role as a complete package. Our goal is to help you be a great board member!

Board Bound Leadership is valuable to ensure all current and future board members have a level of competency to be an asset to any organization. It focuses on and addresses the specific capabilities and needs of an organization's board of directors ensuring they understand their unique role in relationship to the four key areas required to lay a strong foundation for organizational success. The key areas include:

- Leadership
- Governance
- Assessment
- Fundraising

Even though each organization is unique it is essential that every board understand the foundation to build systems that match the specific needs. To know what is in alignment and what is not; to understand when their actions will enhance or hurt the organization; to explore their strengths and how to best use them for the organization. But first, let's break some barriers and bust some myths.

Board Bound Leadership is a culmination of many years of witnessing organization after organization struggle with the same issue – board members not equipped with the knowledge needed. So, we knew we had to create a resource, one that presented the fundamental building blocks and first steps to fulfill their role effectively. Our goal for *Board Bound Leadership* is:

1. To identify key issues unique to the nonprofit sector in a strategic way
2. To map out the areas that every board should focus on and create strategies and systems to effectively implement them

3. To provide a system to train and educate all boards on their roles and responsibilities

4. To relieve individual organizations from the training task, allowing them to focus on their mission

To get started, first let's understand the situation. It is not generally a matter of complacency. Most board members want to do their job and really would like to be an asset. If they don't, they are not the right person in the first place. However, they must be exposed to and gain understanding of this unique sector and not rely on long held stereotypical perceptions. Professionals in the sector talk about it, and research has identified what is called "Charity Think," "Poverty Mindset," or the "Tin Cup Mentality" that permeates the sector. Leader adaptability, listed as one of the sectors' top three challenges behind fundraising and marketing, is an area that we must address because a resistance to change in an ever-changing environment will ultimately negatively impact developing effective strategies. We're sure you've heard statements like this:

- "But we've always done it this way."
- "Somehow we'll get by – we usually do."
- "We're doing pretty well this year."

We must **STOP** this train of thought. It is our goal to transform boards that accept the status quo and make statement like these, to raise the bar and strive to be a great organization.

What do great boards look like?

Some nonprofit boards seem to "have their act together" while others are far from it. Some boards have an excellent relationship with the executive director, their meetings run smoothly and are productive, and board members are truly engaged in the mission of the organization. At the other end of the spectrum there are boards that are disorganized, unclear about their roles and responsibilities, micromanage the executive director, or are disconnected from the mission. What is the secret of a high-functioning board of directors? Is it the actual board members? Is it the board training? Is there some sort of "secret sauce" for boards?

Boards must balance their role as oversight bodies with their role as forces supporting the organization. Boards must exercise their fiduciary duties with care, and recognize that good governance is about more than checklists. Good governance is about providing critical capital, intellect, reputation, resources, access, and be the force behind nonprofit success and thereby strengthen communities.

It's More Than Being Responsible – It's Being the Steward

> ### STEWARD LEADER
> *"Recognizes the human and material resources in their care and ACTS to <u>nurture and develop</u> these and maintains momentum in pursuit of a mission."*

Responsible boards are competent stewards focusing on fiduciary oversight, making sure their organizations comply with the law, acting with financial integrity, and operating effectively and ethically. Exceptional boards add active engagement and independent decision making to the oversight function. Their members are open and honest with each other and the chief executive. They passionately challenge and support each others' efforts in pursuit of the mission. The difference between exceptional boards and those that are merely responsible lies in thoughtfulness and intentionality, action and engagement, knowledge, and communication.

Nonprofit board members face higher expectations and greater scrutiny than ever before. This increased scrutiny comes from the media, government, and from all levels of the community. The public is

22

demanding to know more about what goes on in boardrooms. All of this points to the importance of being very clear about the roles and responsibilities of nonprofit board members.

Most board members want to be part of a board with a high bar of excellence, one that is knowledgeable about its duties and conducting itself in a way that

Set the bar high,
Then aim higher

enhances the value, effectiveness, and credibility of their organization. The best place to start is solid board recruitment and training so everyone is operating with the same playbook and working together with a common understanding of their function.

It is critical to develop a high performing board that board members understand the difference between being a leader and accepting board members' responsibilities, versus being a manager, which is the staff's task. A comprehensive job description for board members helps minimize any ambiguities about expectations. The board's legal authority and the responsibilities of its individual members are distinct yet interdependent. Finding and walking that fine line can be tricky sometimes but it is possible if everyone understands basic board roles, responsibilities, and function. Board members must know when to put on their board hat.

When determining board qualifications, it is not a one size fits all formula. There are several factors to consider such as the size of your organization's staff, whether it is a true membership organization whose board members are elected by the members, whether board membership is politically appointed, or whether certain qualities are mandated by your bylaws (for example board members must represent the segment of population the organization serves). These factors will help determine where emphasis needs to placed. If your organization has mandated membership, it will be a challenge to address these issues covered in this book. Many groups choose to have strong committee structures with members outside the board. However, no matter which type of board your organization adopts or needs the four essential elements of leadership, governance, assessment, and fundraising presented in *Board Bound Leadership* are universal elements that boards are held accountable for. Gaining a high level of understanding of these components often is the result of a well-organized, clear board training program led by an outside entity.

What to Expect

Board Bound Leadership was created to be the primer and go to resource to gain and implement the fundamental elements of board leadership. We have identified four areas that are the essence of a board member's role and responsibilities and that are essential for organizational success. Is this book a be all and end all resource? Absolutely not, we live in an ever-changing environment and we also believe in continuous improvement and building a culture of learning. This should be the first step and should be reviewed annually.

We realize that every board is different and some may need more in the way of understanding the nonprofit sector, so we've provided in the appendix additional information on the legal regulations, start up requirements other topics for those organizations in their infancy stages that perhaps don't even have nonprofit status yet.

Likewise, there are a few nonprofits for which fundraising is not an issue, but they are the exception to the rule. If you're with one of those organizations, you can adapt the fundraising section accordingly.

But first, let's bust some myths about the sector.

BOARD BOUND LEADERSHIP *NOTES*

CHAPTER 3

BUSTING THE MYTHS

Why is it important that we address myths? Because myths can have a serious negative impact, block progress, and impede the success of organizations. On a regular basis, we are totally astonished by how many hold these myths to be true and willing to defend their belief – *belief,* not fact. Therefore, so we can all be on the same page it is important to explore the most common myths and get the facts.

There are so many myths floating around about nonprofit organizations and the entire sector. These myths are related to careers, operations, programs, basically all aspects of the sector. Many of the myths impact organizational growth and sometimes even cause damage. As we all know, or maybe you don't, a myth is a story that everyone believes, but is not true. So here we have assembled some of the most widely-accepted myths that have been circulated by some of the largest organizations across the country. We are going to do some myth busting and hopefully shed some light on how they got started but more

important why they are not true. First we will explore some sector myths and then address those specific to board application.

General Myths

1. **MYTH - Nonprofits can't make a profit.**

   It's wrong for a nonprofit to have more money than they immediately need. The best a nonprofit should hope for is to break even, and if they do run a profit, they should not be fundraising.

   > **MYTH BUSTER**: To the contrary, a nonprofit with operating reserves can invest in a more sustainable organization, conduct evaluations to make sure their solution is the best one, recruit a highly competent staff, and weather economic fluctuations. For a donor, it is far better to invest in an organization with the people and systems necessary to effectively tackle a social problem than an organization that is barely getting by. The best nonprofits are those that create a financial model that allows them the money mix (revenue, capital, reserves) necessary to make the best decisions and invest where and when they must. Remember that part we told you about from the IRS code-- what makes a nonprofit a nonprofit, is that no profits inure to an individual or group of individuals! Profit is fine, in fact it's great, as long as it is being put back into serving the organization's mission.

2. **MYTH - There are too many nonprofits.**

   Oh, we hear this so often (mostly by funders) that there are "too many" nonprofits. Does anyone complain about how many banks, restaurants, dry cleaners, etc. there are in the community? In the United States, and other capitalist countries, we believe that competition is healthy. This myth comes from the fact that the sector is undercapitalized which causes organizations to compete for scarce resources.

MYTH BUSTER: Let's fix that problem instead. There are times when it makes sense to bring two nonprofits that address similar needs together to save costs, but that's usually the exception not the rule. The process of merging two organizations is itself incredibly time-intensive and costly, and, honestly, rarely do funders invest the amount of resources required to ensure a successful merger. Every nonprofit should regularly assess how they fit into the external market place of social problems and competitors working on similar problems. If a nonprofit determines that it is no longer adding unique value to that marketplace, then they should reorganize, merge, or disband, whichever makes most strategic sense.

3. **MYTH - Nonprofits, unlike businesses, are inefficient.**

   This myth takes many forms: "nonprofits are too slow," "nonprofits should sell more products or services,", "nonprofits should run more like a business," and the list goes on. The underlying assumption is that the for-profit world is inherently smarter, more strategic, nimbler, and more effective.

   MYTH BUSTER: The truth is that all three sectors (business, government, and nonprofit) have their stars (like Apple), their screw ups (like Lehman Brothers) and a multitude in between. In fact, 50 percent of startup businesses fail in the first two years. Not true for nonprofits. Inefficiency in the nonprofit sector is merely a symptom of a larger problem, also present in other sectors. Areas such as insufficient training, lack of adequate capital to fund enough of the right staff, technology, systems, evaluation, and marketing required to address the intractable problems nonprofits are trying to solve. Let's talk about that instead.

4. **MYTH - Nonprofits are outside the economy and do not contribute to it.**

This myth is a perspective which negatively impacts internally and externally creating an opinion of perceived worth of the sector. The myth is that nonprofits are not a critical component of our economic system.

> **MYTH BUSTER**: Fact – the nonprofit sector is the third largest workforce behind retail and manufacturing and employs 10.2 percent or 2.24 million people in the US and accounts for 5.4 percent of GDP. Also, the number of nonprofits grew 25 percent from 2001-2011, while the number of businesses only grew by 0.5 percent. As government continues to slough off services to nonprofits, those numbers will only continue to grow. The nonprofit sector is not tangential to the economy, but rather an instrumental part of it. Nonprofits that have done an economic impact study are usually themselves surprised at their contributions to the community in the form of salaries goods and services purchases, and auxiliary contributions to the community in the form of stimulating the economy.

5. **MYTH - A well-run nonprofit should have low "overhead" costs.**

Somewhere in the twilight zone some watchdog group, or perhaps a funder that was trying to validate their giving made an arbitrary statement assigning first 15 percent, then 25 percent as a cap for all operating cost. Not taking into consideration that "operating" cost for different organizations cannot be based on a one size fits all formula.

> **MYTH BUSTER**: Reality: Operating costs, such as paying utility bills, rent, salaries, and investing in office equipment are referred to by a variety of names, including "overhead," "administrative costs," and "indirect costs." While the terminology varies, one thing does not: these costs are essential

to delivering on a nonprofit's mission, and have a direct relation to the level of effectiveness or the outcomes a charitable nonprofit may deliver. Nonprofits are encouraged to educate funders and donors about the true costs of delivering services. If your nonprofit requires higher overhead costs to deliver services, show your supporters how those core infrastructure costs are essential and advancing your mission. A new nonprofit will almost always have a higher overhead just as a new business has start-up costs that will decrease over time.

6. **Myth - Nonprofits have no role in politics and can't lobby.** The myth is that charity is too noble to be mired in the mess of pushing for political change. Yes, tax-exempt charitable nonprofit organizations are *not* permitted to engage in partisan political activity, such as supporting or opposing any candidate for public office.

> **MYTH BUSTER**: The fact is that simply providing services is no longer enough to solve the underlying problems. Nonprofits are increasingly recognizing that they can no longer sit by and watch their client load increase while disequilibrium grows. Nonprofits must (and already are) advocate for changes to the ineffective systems that produce the need for their existence. There is a difference between lobbying and advocating. Every charitable nonprofit can and should make its voice heard on issues that are important to its mission and to the people or cause the nonprofit serves. As advocates, nonprofits are allowed to speak to issues that benefit or harm their cause.

7. **Myth - Most nonprofits are large and have many resources.**
This myth is perpetuated because of visibility and the nonprofit we most hear about are the larger organizations.

MYTH BUSTER: In fact, 82.5 percent of most nonprofits have small budgets, annual revenue of under one million dollars, and small numbers of employees. While large, well known nonprofits, such as the Red Cross, have high visibility, those nonprofits are not representative of the charitable nonprofit community.

8. **Myth - Nonprofit employees should be paid less than people in other sectors.**

Perpetuated by a belief organizations are not making a profit or should be run by volunteers.

MYTH BUSTER: Staff who run nonprofits should be paid salaries equal to what they would earn in the for-profit world. As we stated previously, what makes a nonprofit a nonprofit, per the IRS, is that no individual or group of individuals is making a profit on the organizations' surplus of funds. Remember that staff members in nonprofits are performing the same type of jobs that staff in a for-profit are doing—developing and delivering programs and services, bookkeeping, serving as CEO, etc. and they should be fairly compensated for this work. Many CEOs of nonprofits are running multi-million dollar organizations!

A paid staff represents credibility and viability of a nonprofit organization. Don't confuse having paid staff with the legal stipulation of a volunteer board. It is comparing apples and oranges. In fact, many grantors rank your viability and ability to successfully carry out a project based on having paid staff and will not even consider an application if there is no paid staff to ensure accountability.

Board Specific Myths

1. **Myth: Before serving, you must have a deep understanding of the nonprofit's work.**

Myth Buster: You're not going to know everything, ever – and that's OK. There's a lot to learn about a nonprofit's work and the nonprofit sector in general. From funding sources, to the specific services the nonprofit offers, each nonprofit has an unending list of things you can learn in order to become an asset as a board member. You will not know everything at the beginning however you can be an effective advocate for the nonprofit. Just start with the basics. Become familiar with the nonprofit's history, memorize its mission statement, talk about its impact in the community, and be able to align it with ways a possible donor or volunteer can contribute to its work.

2. **Myth: You have to be an executive or high-level leader.**

    Myth Busting: As we have mentioned, a nonprofit board consist of members with a wide range of diverse backgrounds and experience. That is why the sector is so unique. Good nonprofits are more interested in building diverse, inclusive boards than placing only high-level executives on their boards. After all, boards that consist of individuals with a variety of skills, perspectives and community connections can offer more innovation and insight to the organization they serve.

3. **Myth: The best size for a board is 16.**

    Myth Busting: Well, that's the average size. (Do you want to be average?) There isn't a "best" size for a board. Research shows that small boards think they should be bigger and big board's think they should be smaller. We often recommend an odd number of members, five, seven etc… to accommodate determining a majority on an action item. Size should be determined by needs and over time may change. But as a baseline consider items such as:

    - What the organization needs the board to do at this time in its history.
    - How many people the executive director and the staff can support?
    - The size of the room at your organization where the board meets (really!).

4. **Myth: The annual approval of the budget is the cornerstone of the board's financial oversight.**

    Myth Busting: Budget approval is often a meaningless act because most of the time board members aren't familiar enough with details to know whether the income is accurately projected and the expenses represent sound choices. Instead the annual budget approval process should be viewed as a way to offer guidelines to staff for where the organization needs to be financially at the end of the year. This will promote (we hope) self monitoring and focus throughout the year rather than trying to ferret out details in a complex budget before voting to approve it.

5. **Myth: Boards are supposed to raise money.**

    Myth Busting: Nonprofits are required by law to have boards (as are for-profit corporations) in order to hold the organization accountable to the public (not to raise money). And, in addition, boards don't raise money, board *members* raise money.

    The board approves a plan for how the organization will obtain funds (in its approval of the budget) through some combination of donations, earned income, grants, etc. Then individual board members will help execute the plan by obtaining donations, making connections for earned income and grants, and so forth.

6. **Myth: We're an all-volunteer organization and we can't accomplish much until we have paid staff.**

    Myth Busting: Many high-impact organizations don't have staff, and will never have staff. All-volunteer organizations (AVOs) often represent the community at its best, and many field hundreds of volunteers every week. If you're an AVO, take pride in what you accomplish, and don't feel that "growing up" needs to mean having paid staff. Remember, each nonprofit organization is unique, and must be structured to meet their specific needs.

7. **Myth: We're too small to do succession planning," or "Our ED isn't going anywhere for awhile."**

⬛ Myth Busting: This myth has implications on several levels. First to often the concept of succession planning is relegated to replacing the executive director. This is a narrow viewpoint. Quality succession planning encompasses all of the areas that strengthen the organizational integrity and its ability to carrying out the mission. No organization should be reliant on one person or specific board composition. Succession planning includes creating organizational documents, systems and processes that support and encourage the ability for anyone to step into a role and fully understand their task. To always have processes in place to either build and groom successors (stewardship) or identify potential candidates. Succession also can also use assessment strategies to measure mission relevancy. Just a couple examples are:

- Making the ED's job do-able (it's hard to replace a superhero, but it's not as hard to replace an excellent executive director)
- Ensuring policy documents are created
- Ensure that all those brought on board understand and support the mission.

A True Horror Story Full of Myths and Misconceptions

In our years of service we have heard some real horror stories from the field. Unfortunately the following passage is a true scenario that was shared with us. It made us quiver in our shoes and really drove home what we have believed for so long is true. Myths and misconceptions are perpetuated from a lack of knowledge on all levels. Here's the story.

My consultant told me after a board retreat, "Fire that board member." I was shocked when he said this! As a new executive director of a small nonprofit in the Midwest, I was on a tight schedule of program and fund development. I needed all hands on deck, especially my lead volunteer! But, this board member did not agree with the goals established by the nonprofit and despite the fact he was my strongest volunteer, he did not respect me. The consultant said, "he needs to go. If you do not fire him, he will undermine your leadership publicly and privately."

This board member's excuse to not give financially was because he felt that his many hours of volunteering was his contribution This made it impossible to enforce 100 percent board giving. Note: He was the interim ED until I was hired and he had a controlling personality. Red Flags all over the place! But, he went to my church so I let it all go. I did not heed the consultant's advice, hoping to work with him and encourage better behavior when two years later, the chair position of our board was open, he was swiftly voted in despite my warnings, because no one else had "time" to serve or was too new on the board to qualify. Lacking respect for women in leadership, and desiring to change the course of the organizations growth plan, he called an emergency secret, private meeting with a quorum while our organization's founder was incapacitated, and voted me out. Within twenty-four hours, I was let go from my job.

Heed the warnings of wise counsel, you must fire board members who don't see the larger vision, who do not contribute financially, or support you as a leader. Someone will be leaving the organization and if you don't act, it will be you! And, it may hurt the entire organization.

If an organization's board leadership lacks vision, has poor communication, and has no desire to connect with all its constituents, the organization itself will fail, unless it can find qualified leadership.

Within this passage there are several misguided concepts that we need to address. You might have recognized them already.

Issue: Lack of and Misplaced Leadership = Major Fail.

Our thoughts: There are several sub issues within this story that for us were the proverbial *red flags*. First this is an executive director explaining how they didn't heed the advice of a consultant to 'fire' a board member. Executive directors can't fire a board member! However the entire passage is an indicator of a much bigger problem. The board was not carrying out its responsibilities. It had relinquished its responsibilities to the ED, had allowed a bully to dictate his rules, had not addressed festering problems, and then the ultimate blow was being totally complacent in selecting leadership.

Yes, the ED did not understand her role, power and position however the board failed her. Yes failed her by allowing the ED to assume the authoritative position regarding board matters, by not providing a clear job description, and by not conducting an annual performance assessment. And that's only how it failed *her*.

37

It failed the organization by not carrying out individual responsibilities as board members. Individual board members' inaction and ignoring their roles and responsibilities related to leadership, governance, assessment, and fundraising negatively impacted the entire organization. We are sad this is a true story but we hope in the future the scenario will be quite different.

Final Note

This is just a short example of the some of the beliefs that can really have a negative impact on the effectiveness of an organization. It is important to keep in mind just like every other industry times change, advancements are made, and best practices shift. One of the top three challenges identified in the nonprofit sector was *Leader Adaptability*. It is up to the leaders and visionaries to stay up to date and current on what are facts and what is a myth.

CHAPTER 4

$\mathcal{U}$sing the Modules

In the next four chapters we will explore the four key essentials of leadership, governance, assessment, and fundraising. We will continue to bust myths but more importantly provide readers with the framework to become a great board member.

Before getting started it is important to note that each module is presented and explored from the individual board member's point of view. We say this because it is important for you the reader to make sure you have made the paradigm shift, to change the hat you are wearing to *being* and *thinking* like a board member. Shifting to this role as a board member is important because being a board member is a unique perspective, especially if you have served in other capacities within the sector such as staff member or volunteer. The goal, focus and even mindset required in those positions are different than that of being a board member.

So, here's what you can expect and how to get the most out of each module.

Format

Each module is presented in a straight forward structure and design and contains the following elements,

- Baseline quiz – to assess current understanding
- Content Goal – what we are trying to accomplish
- Essential Concepts – the what and why of that module
- Notes – to track your thoughts
- Action Steps – map out a plan for you or your organization's growth

Baseline Quiz

We begin with a quiz to help you determine current proficiencies but to also highlight some perceived beliefs that might need to be updated or shifted. It is a valuable tool to assess an

Answers for quizzes available in Appendix

individual's baseline level of understanding and perhaps initially identify gaps, but more important it is hoped that it will open the reader's eyes to all of the essential elements that needs to be understood and focused on within that module.

Content Goal

Drawing upon Victoria's extensive education and training background it is essential to identify and understand what goal is desired. They may seem simplistic but for some readers this will be the first time they have seen the goal identified.

The Essentials

The four essentials are the heart of the book and results of why we wrote it. Each module is the roadmap for that area and with any map you can follow the main course of direction or take numerous side trips enhancing the journey. We say this to emphasize even though this is a solid representation of a board members' role and responsibilities there will be many *side trips* based on the nature of your organization.

Notes

You've probably already noticed and it's pretty self explanatory that at the end of each chapter we've included a *BBL Notes page*. We want you to use this book as *your* foundation builder and as a works in progress tool. We've all had those brilliant ideas or aha moments pop in our head, sparked by a passage or statement, joint them down for future action. Your notes can become your why, refer to them often and let them help you develop your skills.

Action Plan

We hope you will take the opportunity to map out your action steps and to celebrate your accomplishments. We'd love to hear about some of your results.

To get a digital copy of the action plan document visit:

http://BBLeaders.com/action-plan

Let's get started!

CHAPTER 5

MODULE ONE
LEADERSHIP QUIZ

This simple True – False quiz will assess you as a board member and your beliefs related to a board member's role. Answer questions from you own perspective, understanding, and point of view.

	Individual Assessment: *Answer from a personal perspective*	T	F
1	I understand and support the mission of the organization.		
2	I am knowledgeable about the organization's programs and services.		
3	I follow trends and important developments related to this organization.		
4	I assist with fundraising and give a significant annual gift to the organization.		
5	I read and understand the organization's financial statements.		
6	I have a good working relationship with the chief executive.		
7	I recommend individuals for service to this board.		
8	I prepare for and participate in board meetings and committee meetings.		
9	I act as a good-will ambassador to the organization.		
10	I find serving on the board to be a satisfying and rewarding experience.		
	Board Leadership Assessment: *Answer from your perspective of the board as a whole*		
11	It's the responsibility of the board to manage the executive director.		
12	A board's responsibilities include management of the organization.		
13	Getting things done is more important than developing the road ahead.		

14	Board leadership has nothing to do with the strategic planning.		
15	Our role is not to motivate and nurture, but to set policy and guidelines.		
16	As a board we must protect the mission so it never changes.		
17	Our role is more to ask, listen, and learn, than to be an authority.		
18	Our role is to plan for change on a regular basis.		
19	A leader needs to avoid showing vulnerability to his or her peers.		
20	As a board, we are responsible for all aspects of the organization.		

Scorecard in the appendix.

$\mathcal{L}$eadership

Goal: To define and identify leadership qualities and skills required in the nonprofit sector.

"A leader's job is not to do the work for others, it's to help others figure out how to do it themselves, to get things done, and to succeed beyond what they thought possible."

Simon Sinek

Leadership in the nonprofit sector and especially as a member of the board of directors requires unique skill sets. As the leader, you must create the current foundation, and be the visionary to plan for the future and legacy of the organization. You must understand your role and responsibilities as a steward leader and protector. As a steward leader, you are the catalyst for change and depend on your own power to make others powerful. Stewardship is a collective attribute that is not personality or people based but embedded in the process. A steward leader recognizes the human and material resources in their care and *acts* to nurture and develop them while maintaining momentum focused on a mission.

Know Your Role

Those that have the privilege to be selected to sit on a nonprofit board of directors are charged with a unique role. They are the keepers of the vision and automatically step into a leadership position. Therefore, before we explore the qualities of great leaders let's first make sure you understand the difference between being a manager and being a leader. This is extremely important because in working with many boards over the years we've witnessed individuals acting as managers and this became an obstacle that not only created tension within the organization but also blocked progress. It is important, especially for "working boards" (a term which we personally despise, because most often it means that the board is managing, not governing) to know when to switch hats from being a volunteer to being the leader and what's the difference.

The traditional view of management assumes that a manager's job is to keep the machine running smoothly. In this world view, the people on the manager's team are essentially machine parts.

They are interchangeable. Once they are hired into a role, their job is to perform that role (to run their piece of the machine) according to goals and standards that preceded them and that will outlast their tenure in the job. The presumption is that the machine is more important and more powerful than anyone who helps to run it.

Leadership, especially in the nonprofit sector, must take the opposite view! The energy on your team powers everything you will accomplish. The machine can and should change whenever it makes sense to change it, even many times a day as long as the change is mission driven. When was the last time you assessed the effectiveness of your machine, maybe it's time to junk the machine and invent something totally new. This chart is a simple comparison of roles for managers and leaders.

Leaders allow people to design their own jobs as much as possible and to put their own stamp on their jobs. A leader is not working to achieve machine-like process perfection to be repeated over and over until the end of time. People are creative. Machines in general are not.

MANAGERS	LEADERS
Focus on things	Focuses on people
Does things right	Does the right thing
Plans	Inspires
Organizes	Influences
Directs	Motivates
Controls	Builds
Follows rules	Shapes Entities

Unfortunately, in a 2014 report from the *National Center for Nonprofit Statistics*, one of the top three challenges nonprofits face is a lack of leader adaptability. Does your organization show symptoms of the "We've always done it this way" syndrome?

Who can get excited about doing the same thing day after day, year after year, to no visible end? There must be more to the mission than that, and part of a leader's job is to explore and exalt the connections between his or her team's mission and each team member's personal mission. They will all know what

We cannot solve our problems with the same thinking we used when we created them.- Albert Einstein

the mission is and know their piece and value to accomplish it. Without a mission, there is no place to lead your team toward! Without a mission, where are you headed?

Leading by example and leading by empowering people are the hallmarks of action-based leadership. Just as managers have subordinates and leaders have followers, managers create circles of power while leaders create circles of influence. Leadership refers to an individual's ability to influence, motivate, and enable others to contribute toward organizational success. Influence and inspiration separate leaders from managers, not power and control.

In India, M. K. Gandhi inspired millions of people to fight for their rights, and he walked shoulder to shoulder with them so India could achieve independence in 1947. His vision became everyone's dream and ensured that the country's push for independence was unstoppable. The world needs leaders like him who can think beyond problems, have a vision, and inspire people to convert challenges into opportunities, a step at a time.

Think about this the next time you are in a board meeting. When the discussion stops focusing on the tasks at hand — and talk shifts to the vision, purpose, and aspirations instead, that's when you will recognize you are among a group of leaders.

Pulling It All Together for the Nonprofit Sector

Over many years of reviewing leadership across sectors and industries, what evolved and designed specifically for the nonprofit sector was an *Intentional Leadership* model. This model makes the assumption that individuals come with the intentions and desire to nurture not only an organization but the people within it. It is based on skills and thought patterns which are designed partially from the good to great philosophy, plus best practices for the nonprofit sector. Intentional Leadership Model is based on four fundamental concepts of a leader's role which consist of:

1. **Caretaker:** Holder of the Vision and Values
2. **Conductor:** Create Collaboration and Innovation
3. **Champion:** Influence, Inspire, Advocate, and Celebrate
4. **Controller:** Responsibility and Accountability

These attributes are the cornerstone of what is needed from you as a board member. Some will come naturally others you will need to make a conscious effort to shift your way of thinking and actions. The important element is to recognize leadership is most effective when taught via example – walk the talk. In the long run, you will not only be equipped to be a valuable asset to your organization but you will be building its future.

Walk the Talk

In the 1930's there was a young boy who had become addicted to and obsessed with eating sugar. His mother decided to get help and took the long and hot journey with her son walking many miles and hours under the scorching sun. She finally reached Gandhi and asked him to tell her son to stop eating sugar, it wasn't good for his health. Gandhi replied, "I cannot tell him that. But you may bring him back in a few weeks and then I will talk to him." The mother was confused and upset and took the boy home.

Two weeks later she came back. This time Gandhi looked directly at the boy and said ""Boy, you should stop eating sugar. It is not good for your health." The boy nodded his head and promised he wouldn't. The boy's mother was puzzled. She asked "Why didn't you tell him that two weeks ago when I brought him here to see you?"
Gandhi smiled and said "Mother, two weeks ago I was eating a lot of sugar myself."

BOARD BOUND LEADERSHIP *NOTES*

This is an image of the Action Plan.

To access a digital copy follow this link:

http://BBLeaders.com/action-plan

Action Plan

Instructions

This action plan will help identify areas you want to improve, strengthen, or gain skills and knowledge to support being a great board member. By creating a personal action plan it will make you accountable to yourself and the organization you serve.

Initially only select three areas – more than that makes it feel overwhelming. As you complete a step – Celebrate. Then move on to the next step on the list. As areas are completed, add new ones to always remain in a cycle of continuous improvement and learning.

Category: [　] Leadership　[　] Governance　　[　] Assessment　　[　] Fundraising

Focus area Skills or knowledge desired	Strategy: Books, training, equipment	Target Date!!
1		
2		
3		

CHAPTER 6

BOARD
BOUND
LEADERSHIP

This quiz will help you get started in determining whether you understand its primary elements of governance. We suggest the governance committee have each board member complete this quiz individually and then compile the results and share with the entire board.

Board Governance Indicators Answer YES or NO		Y	N
1	Members have full and common understanding of their roles and responsibilities		
2	Members understand the organization's missions and its programs.		
3	Members are clear regarding individual and group roles and responsibilities.		
4	Members have clear goals and actions resulting from relevant and realistic strategic planning.		
5	Members attend to policy-related decisions which effectively guide operational activities.		
6	Members receive regular reports on and understand finances/budgets, products/program performance and other important matters.		
7	Members help set fundraising goals and are actively involved in fundraising.		
8	Members effectively represent the organization to the community.		
9	Members meet to facilitate focus and progress on important organizational matters.		
10	Members regularly monitor and evaluate progress on important organizational matters.		
11	Members approve comprehensive volunteer and personnel		

	policies.		
12	Each member of the board feels involved and interested in the board's work.		
13	All necessary skills, stakeholders, and diversity are represented on the board.		

Scorecard in the appendix

Governance

Goal: To identify and clarify the role and responsibilities of nonprofit governance.

"Letting the wrong people hang around is unfair to all the right people, as they inevitably find themselves compensating for the inadequacies of the wrong people. Worse, it can drive away the best people. Strong performers are intrinsically motivated by performance, and when they see their efforts impeded by carrying extra weight, they eventually become frustrated."

James C. Collins

What is Governance?

The formal definition is, *the structures and processes designed to ensure accountability, transparency, responsiveness, rule of law, stability, equity and inclusiveness, empowerment, and broad-based participation.*

Taking it a step further, governance is the process of providing strategic leadership to a nonprofit organization. It entails the functions of setting direction, making policy and strategy decisions, overseeing and monitoring organizational performance, and ensuring overall accountability. Boards are generally led by an executive committee that consists of four officers in most cases- president (or chair), vice president (or vice chair), secretary and treasurer. In this description please note the word *manage* is not used and it is important to make the distinction of manager and leader in governance.

> *Get Rid of Your Nominating Committee!* Instead of a nominating committee that meets once a year to fill vacant seats, try a year-round board committee. (It can be called the governance committee or the committee on directorship or any name the organization feels comfortable with.)

Structure and Process

Because of there are a wide range of types of nonprofit organizations naturally there will be various organizational structures. Some structures are more effective and a better fit to serve the needs of the organization. When deciding on or even exploring a shift to a new structure for your organizational governing body one key criteria is organizational capacity, how many people are or will be actively engaged in the board's processes? For our purposes, we will compare two different structures the *traditional* and *three tiered* formats with each offering different benefits.

Traditional Organizational Structure

The most commonly known and probably most often used is the traditional format as shown in this diagram. It is comprised of the standard committees of fundraising, finance, nominating, and programs. Each assigned specific task and goals. This structure is effective if 1) the organization has sufficient capacity and 2) there is sufficient operational

Traditional Nonprofit Organizational Structure

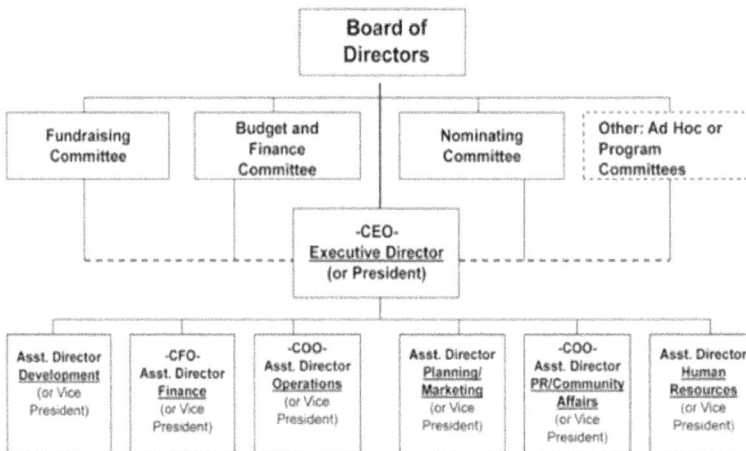

```
                        ┌─────────────────┐
                        │   Board of      │
                        │   Directors     │
                        └─────────────────┘

┌──────────────┐  ┌──────────────┐  ┌──────────────┐  ┌──────────────┐
│ Fundraising  │  │  Budget and  │  │  Nominating  │  │ Other: Ad Hoc│
│ Committee    │  │   Finance    │  │  Committee   │  │ or Program   │
│              │  │  Committee   │  │              │  │ Committees   │
└──────────────┘  └──────────────┘  └──────────────┘  └──────────────┘

                        ┌─────────────────┐
                        │     -CEO-       │
                        │ Executive Dir.  │
                        │ (or President)  │
                        └─────────────────┘
```

| Asst. Director Development (or Vice President) | -CFO- Asst. Director Finance (or Vice President) | -COO- Asst. Director Operations (or Vice President) | Asst. Director Planning/ Marketing (or Vice President) | -COO- Asst. Director PR/Community Affairs (or Vice President) | Asst. Director Human Resources (or Vice President) |

support. What this means generally the organization is well established with boards that consist of 15 or more members because the policy is often to require all members of each committee to be active board members. This structure is also most effective if there is a dedicated staff managing day to day operations, systems and programs. The committees work independently on a very specific task making it necessary to put effort towards or have support to align projects. Another drawback we've come across on a regular basis when using this structure, the committees don't feel they need to meet regularly but only when their reports or services are needed. However, because this structure is the one most people are familiar with, they automatically think it is the only *acceptable* format. A board should create systems that meet their own specific needs – not vice versa. As you will come to recognize as we go through the other modules, supportive elements such as marketing are not addressed on the board level or integrated into the system.

Three-tiered Structure

The three-tiered format is gaining more acceptance, especially for new or smaller organizations because of the benefits it provides beyond a solid governance format. The three committees consist of internal, external, and governance and the goals are to align task that crossover several areas, to have task ongoing versus by cycles, and to make it manageable, especially for small boards. It also encourages inviting community members to participate on the committee level in that the bylaws would require only that the chair be a board member. The chair would create a committee from membership or other viable resources to represent the organization in fulfilling committee responsibilities. The scope of each committee includes,

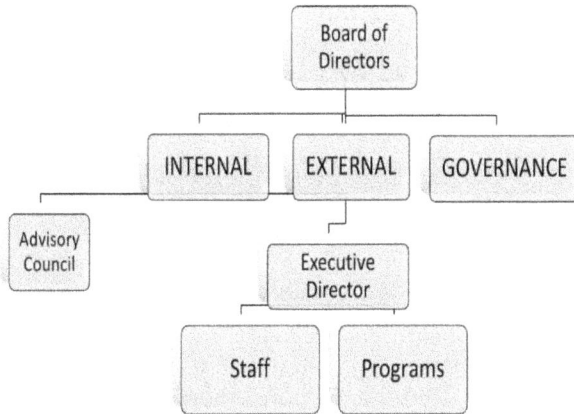

- **Internal Affairs**: All internal and operational issues which include those related to finance, human resources, and facilities

- **External Affairs**: All external issues which include fundraising, public relations, and marketing are the committee responsibility.

- **Governance Committee**: Responsible for the health and functioning of the board. It recruits new members, conducts orientation, produces board materials, and evaluates the performance of the board itself. It is responsible for ensuring the effectiveness of the current board and for recruiting tomorrow's leaders.

Executive Committee

There can be an executive committee that also has a slightly different makeup. This executive committee could consist of the board's officers and the chairs from each of the three standing committees. Deciding on which organizational structure is most effective for your needs is important.

Advisory Council

In the three-tiered structure diagram an advisory council is included because it is often formed as another way to gain community support without the obligation of being a board member. Its composition should be determined by the board of directors and key stakeholders based on strategic planning and to best fit and meet the current and long term goals.

Defining Role versus Responsibilities

ROLE

- Governance is primary role—*not* management
- Roles are defined via committee or position and include fundraising, being an ambassador, hiring/firing/*supporting* the executive director

RESPONSIBILITIES

- Understand and govern aspects of the organizations systems that support the mission.
- Financial accountability
- Legal compliance

Role of the Board of Directors

1. Keep organization clean and legal – *Best Business Practices*

   - Oversee financial and risk management.
   - Ensure all legal filings are maintained
   - Monitor organizational performance.

> **Beyond Governance**
>
> *An effective group spirit on a board is one that attracts its members, makes them want to work with one another, and gives them a sense of pride and satisfaction in the program and the board itself.*

2. Serve as a link to the outside community – *Building Resources*

- Clearly understand the mission and the scope of organization's programming to fulfill the mission.
- Assist in board development through relationship building and cultivation of future board members.
- Build the organizations reputation and be an advocate in the community.
- Provide expertise and access for organizational needs.

3. Define the organization's future – *Strategic Planning*
   - Participate in and approve strategic and policy decisions.
   - Hire and monitor executive director's performance.
   - Participate in evaluating and improving board performance.
   - Ensure adequate resources through contributing on an annual basis by volunteering, donating, and promoting volunteerism and philanthropy in our community.

4. Come with Qualifications – *Contribute for Success*
   - Recognized member of the community with proven leadership skills and outstanding community contacts.
   - Ability to fulfill time commitment to the board beyond attending monthly board meetings.
   - Willing and able to support with resources by advocating in the community about the mission, by volunteering, promoting volunteerism, and by donating and promoting philanthropy.

Board Officers Roles

Chairperson	Vice Chairperson
• Spokesperson for the board	• Takes over chair function in the event of absence, incapacity, or death
• Presides at meetings	
• Serves /leads members	• May be assigned other specific functions by the chair
• Primary contact for inside leadership	
	• Traditional chair of planning

	committee
• Motivates by example, and holds members accountable • Principle supervisor for the ex. director	
Secretary	**Treasurer**
• Cares for and keeps official corporate records, minutes, archives • Responsible for taking minutes at meetings of the board, or approving minutes taken by a staff person	• Custodian of corporate funds, oversees personnel performing accounting functions • Disburses funds as authorized by the board or other constitutional authority • Analyzes fiscal reports, making regular and timely reports to the board • Reports and monitors IRS and state compliance requirements

Additional officers may be defined in the organizational bylaws, but they are not required.

Board of Director's Responsibilities

A. Program

- Understanding each program and how it implements the mission of the organization.
- Approving annual program plans
- Agreeing on methods for program evaluation.

B. Planning

- Define a desired future (vision) for the organization and the means to achieve it.
- Decide mission of the organization and its service population.
- Design the structure and functions necessary to carry out the business and programs effectively and efficiently.
- Ensure that there is always a board approved three-year plan in place to guide decisions and provide focus for the organization.
- Ensure the objectives and action steps are measurable and

monitored for progress.

C. Financial Management
- Approve annual budget
- Monitor budget through fiscal reports, taking action as needed to ensure a balanced budget.
- Obtain and approve an annual audit resulting in an unqualified opinion.
- Oversee investments
- Periodically review insurance coverage to ensure that assets are protected

D. Financial Development
- Establish a financial development (fundraising) plan
- Contribute to the organization (Give first!)
- Support annual giving appeal, special fundraising events, capital campaigns
- Help identify and solicit donors, sell tickets, attend events

E. Human Resources
- Determine the need for an executive director (CEO)
- Develop the executive director (CEO) job description
- Hire and supervise the executive director
- Ensure compliance with laws regarding employers
- Approve policies for affirmative action, personnel
- Assist staff in policy development, legal compliance, studies on personnel strategies.

F. Marketing and Public Relations
- Know the organization's priority constituencies and how effectively the organization is reaching/serving each

- Serve as a knowledgeable advocate for the organization in the community
- Link the organization to external markets
- Ensure that an annual report is prepared and presented

G. Information and Technology Support
- Establish management information system with the technological and software support to ensure its effectiveness
- Help staff determine what information is needed, in what form, when, and for whom in order to make informed decisions

H. Board Affairs
- Define the board size and makeup
- Ensure the continuity of the board
- Evaluate the effectiveness and efficiency of the board, and make appropriate action to improve them

I. Governance - approve bylaws in accordance with state and federal law, to include:
- Qualifications and duties of trustees (directors)
- Composition and terms of the board
- Definition of quorum
- Decision making powers of the board and executive director
- Conflict of interest statements
- Annual cycle of meetings, fiscal year
- Indemnification clause
- Bylaw amendment procedure
- Role and responsibilities of officers, standing committees

Financial and Legal Compliance

Nonprofits must practice sound financial management and comply with a diverse array of legal and regulatory requirements. A nonprofit's financial system should assure the accuracy of financial records. The organization's financial resources should be used in furtherance of its charitable purposes. Organizations should conduct periodic reviews to address regulatory and liability concerns.

A. Financial Accountability

1. A nonprofit should operate in accordance with an annual budget which has been approved by the board of directors.
   a. The finance committee should thoroughly review and access the accuracy and feasibility of projected budget.
   b. Check and balance policies should be in place to allow ongoing monitoring and oversight.
   c. A nonprofit should create and maintain financial reports on a timely basis that accurately reflect the financial activity of the organization.
   d. File IRS form 990 annually and maintain detailed account of finances, evidence of compliance with conflict of interest policies and transparency.

2. For nonprofits with annual revenue in excess of $300,000, the accuracy of the financial reports should be subject to an audit by a Certified Public Accountant.
   a. All nonprofit's no matter the size should at least once a year conduct an audit by an impartial third party.

3. Internal financial statements should be prepared no less frequently than monthly, should he provided to the board of directors, and should identify and explain any material variation between actual and budgeted revenues and expenses.
   a. The ED/CEO should provide a report to finance

committee and at each board meeting present a financial report.

4. Organizations should provide employees a confidential means to report suspected financial impropriety or misuse of organization resources.

   a. The whistle blower law now makes it advisable to have a formal policy in place for the administrative staff and board members.

5. Organizations should have written financial policies governing: (a) investment of the assets of the organization, (b) internal control procedures, (c) purchasing practices, (d) unrestricted current net assets and (e) cash reserves.

   a. There should be concrete guidelines established for not only the aforementioned areas but also detailed gift and donation policies and procedures. These include areas such as acceptance of real property, stocks and bonds, investment instruments and beneficiaries to insurance policies.

B. *Legal Compliance and Accountability*

1. Nonprofits must be aware of and comply with all applicable federal, state, and local laws. This may include, but is not limited to, the following activities: complying with laws and regulations related to fundraising, licensing, financial accountability, human resources, lobbying and political advocacy, and taxation.

2. Organizations should periodically assess the need for insurance coverage in light of the nature and extent of the organization's activities and its financial capacity. Coverage should include hut not be limited to general liability insurance and directors' and

officers' liability insurance. A decision to forego general liability or directors' and officers' liability insurance coverage shall be made by the board of directors only and shall be reflected in the minutes of the meeting at which the decision was made.

3. Nonprofits should periodically conduct an internal review of the organization's compliance with known existing legal, regulatory and financial reporting requirements and should provide a summary of the results to the board of directors.

In general, there are four areas that really sum up the role and responsibilities of a nonprofit board of directors and they include,

1. Keep organization clean and legal
   • Oversee financial and risk management.
   • Ensure all legal filings are done
   • Monitor organizational performance.

2. Serve as link to the community
   • Clearly understand the scope to fulfill the mission.
   • Build relationship building and cultivation of future board members.
   • Build reputation and be an advocate in the community.
   • Provide expertise and access for needs

3. Define organization's future
   • Approval of strategic and policy decisions
   • Hiring & monitoring CEO's performance
   • Evaluating and improving board performance
   • Ensuring adequate resources are available
   • Volunteering and donating

4. Qualified to contribute for success

- Recognized leadership skills and outstanding community contacts.
- Ability to fulfill time commitment to the board and organization beyond attending monthly board meetings.
- Willing and able to support with resources: advocating in the community, volunteering and promoting, donating, and promoting philanthropy.

We've given you an example of what is typical. However, each organization is different and should define roles differently according to your needs. Some organizations do not need a large staff, for example. Some have multiple programs, while others focus on just one area. However, all nonprofits need leadership and sustainability.

What are your needs?

- Human Capital
- Strategies for Sustainability
- Leadership
- Program Support

> **Please, please, please don't ever recruit board members this way!**
> *Linda once experienced a board meeting that was the worst example we've ever witnessed of how some organizations recruit board members. It was December. The executive director said toward the end of the meeting, "Well a few of you are coming to the end of your terms on the board, so we need about three new board members. Does anyone have any ideas?" Eek! Linda wanted to scream! What was wrong with this picture? Several things: It was December and the new board members were to be in place in January! The executive director, not a board member, was the one to raise the issue! And there was no thought given to what skills were needed on the board and who the people might be who possess those skills!*

This is an image of the Action Plan.

To access a digital copy follow this link:

http://BBLeaders.com/action-plan

Action Plan

Instructions

This action plan will help identify areas you want to improve, strengthen, or gain skills and knowledge to support being a great board member. By creating a personal action plan it will make you accountable to yourself and the organization you serve.

Initially only select three areas – more than that makes it feel overwhelming. As you complete a step – Celebrate. Then move on to the next step on the list. As areas are completed, add new ones to always remain in a cycle of continuous improvement and learning.

Category: [   ] Leadership   [   ] Governance   [   ] Assessment   [   ] Fundraising

Focus area Skills or knowledge desired	Strategy: Books, training, equipment	Target Date!!
1		
2		
3		

CHAPTER 7

Assessment is one of the key essentials for success. Before we get into this topic, take this quick quiz to identify the areas you believe your organization is currently or should be assessing.

Indicate Yes or No for all the areas you currently conduct assessments.

Needs Assessment	Y	N	Evaluations of:	Y	N
Staff			Board performance and make-up		
Volunteers			Individual board members performance		
Donors			Program(s)		
Sponsors			Marketing		
Clients			Fundraising		
Community			Management		
Partners			Facilities		

Score 10 points for each yes!

*A*ssessment

Goal: To identify assessment required to measure success, growth, and outcomes.

Leadership must exude a spirit of belief in the importance of evaluation.

Deborah Linnell

Types of Assessment

Within the realm of internal and external assessment the most commonly known strategies include what's called *Formative* and *Summative* assessment.

The majority of the data nonprofits generally disseminate to the public is "summative data," (in business terms we call these trailing indicators) information that sums up how awesome a program is at the end of (usually) a year, when everything has been done. This is the type of data

reported out to the community: *"This year, 85 percent of the kids in our program advanced by one grade level in STEM skills."*

However, organizations should compile different forms of assessment gathered from internal and external areas of the organizational machine ad comprised of both formative and summative data.

Formative assessment should be the bulk of the assessments conducted and data collected. The organization and its board should conduct a needs assessment to examine their own gaps in knowledge or understanding of nonprofit leadership or governance, tools needed to perform their role effectively, and outlining expectations and outcomes. Often an organization will create a job description as the baseline requirement establishing performance benchmark indicators to identify needs and filling gaps.

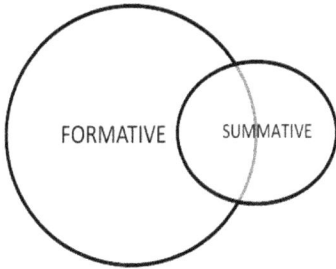

Formative data (also known as leading indicators) could also be categorized as a needs assessment which is a systematic process for determining and addressing needs, or "gaps" between current conditions and desired conditions or wants. The discrepancy between the current condition and wanted condition must be measured to appropriately identify the need. This measurement is valuable in assessing impact. Needs assessments will help answer the what, when, who, and why of planning and development.

> *When the cook tastes the soup that's formative assessment; when the customer tastes the soup, that summative assessment.*

What: Collect information about expressed or implied needs within an area or community.

When: Measurements are conducted early in the exploratory phase of a program or project. In that needs will change with time, it is always beneficial to periodically revisit.

Who: Ideally this includes seeking input from a diverse sample of the stakeholders within the organization and the community at-large. It is also possible to conduct basic needs assessment by yourself or within a team setting as well.

Why: There are a number of reasons you should conduct a needs assessment. Here are just a few…
- Building a program or service that isn't needed/wanted is a waste of time & money
- Keeps the focus on the needs of those being served, not just on what you want to do
- Can uncover things that an outsider might easily miss
- Helps to test assumptions and reduces the risk of doing more harm than good

A program's needs assessment will examine delivery, implementation, assessment of the context, personnel, procedures, etc.

Example: Exercise program for elderly would seek information on activities that are motivating and fun to include in the program.
- What is the definition/scope of the problem/issue, or what's the question?
- What is the problem and how big or serious is it?
- How should the program be delivered to address the problem?
- How well is the program delivered?

Summative assessment or evaluation is at the other end of the spectrum and focuses on the outcomes or impact of a program or project. As mentioned earlier it is the most common type of assessment used and could be used to:

- Examine effects or outcomes
- Summarize describing pre- and post- delivery
- Examine causal effect, overall impact and associated cost

Example: Elderly exercise program evaluation would seek information on improved levels of mobility, participation levels and satisfaction with the program.

- Types: outcome, impact, cost
- Outcomes – what happened?
- Impact – did it create a change?
- Cost-effectiveness/benefit – per person cost related to outcomes.
- Secondary – unexpected results not planned for, both positive and negative

Exploring Internal Assessment

Self-Assessment is the FIRST step to ALL Assessment

As a board, how can you guide others if you can't guide yourself?

Now, let's get to the assessments that you as a board member are likely to get more involved with. Considering the important role the board has within a nonprofit, why would any organization be content with a sub-standard board? An organization should not accept a board with inadequate performance and fulfillment of its responsibilities, and not open and willing to improve its members' individual and collective performance. The best way to make the case for board improvement is to conduct periodic board self-assessments to identify your board's strengths and areas in need of improvement. Why assess performance? Board self-assessment provides you with the opportunity to:

- Look internally at the board itself
- Reflect on your board members' individual and shared responsibilities
- Identify different perceptions and opinions among board members
- Determine areas of responsibility that need attention
- Use the results as a springboard for board improvement
- Increase the level of board teamwork
- Clarify mutual board/staff expectations
- Clarify common objectives as well as check that everyone is speaking the same language, i.e. ensuring that everyone abides by a shared vision
- Demonstrate accountability as a serious organizational value
- Display credibility to funders and other external audiences

A board of director's internal assessment as a whole covers areas which include:
- Board member recruitment to address areas of need
- Leader adaptability to identified needs
- Diversity—ethnic, gender, geographic, age
- Skills and talents—do we have what we need?
- Financial audits and budget projections
- Fundraising
- Using the board grid to understand our needs
- There should also be a self-assessment conducted to identify specific personal needs.
- Job descriptions to establish performance indicator benchmarks
- Understanding organizational needs

Getting Ready - Planning Well is Half the Battle.

Here are some tips that help board members get excited about the assessment process and prepare for it.

Ten Tips to Ensure an Evaluative Culture is Developed

1. Include periodic self-assessment in your bylaws clauses. It is the surest method to make the case for assessment if your bylaws include it as one of the principle policies for the board.
    a. Task the governance committee (not your chief executive or the chair) to ensure that assessment takes place regularly and is well organized. This committee is the permanent structure of your board; officers and chief executives change. Also, self-assessment is a board commitment; when the call for action comes from within the team, the "voice" is different.
    b. Keep in mind that it is a board and not organizational assessment. The entire focus is on the board, on its work, structure, and dynamics.

2. Plan to conduct a self-assessment at least every two years. It may be necessary to conduct one every year because some boards change on an annual basis; but remember that you need time to implement any potential changes and learn new ways to function as a board.

3. Your auditing firm, as an outside monitor, should also make sure that the processes in the bylaws get respected.

4. Clarify the purpose of self-assessment to everyone. It is not to be judgmental or focus only on weaknesses and negative aspects. Its purpose is to help the board get to the next phase of development. One of its benefits is to act as a planning tool for the board.

5. Discuss the questionnaire your board has chosen to use to make sure everyone is familiar with the process and has a chance to ask detailed questions.

6. Expect confidentiality. Opinions and comments expressed during the process should not be attributed to individual board members but should be shared in the aggregate report. Confidentiality is the only way to ensure that everyone shares honest opinions without a filter or fear of being criticized.

7. If possible, rely on an outside facilitator to collect the completed questionnaires, analyze the comments, and provide the full board with a report. This third-party confidentiality brings an added level of neutrality to the end discussion.

8. Provide each board member with the opportunity to comment on how they assessed their own performance vis-à-vis the full board. It is often quite educational to see the results. Not surprising, but often, board members see themselves in a better light than they see the full board's performance. Although we've often found just the opposite, especially when it comes to assessing their personal contributions to the organization, many board members feel they can, and should, be doing more. Keep in mind that comments and opinions are simply perceptions of board members. There are no wrong answers.

9. Include your chief executive in the process. Even if the chief executive is not a voting member of the board, they work closely with the board and should have an insightful perspective of the board's effectiveness.

10. Make sure that the results of the assessment get shared with the full board and action is taken afterwards.

Final note - No follow up is the worst consequence to self-assessment. For some boards, the first self-assessment experience feels awkward and somewhat daunting. However, if the process and the consequences are accepted, the first assessment should result in a beneficial learning experience. Embarking on a second assessment proves that the board has learned the importance of monitoring its own effectiveness. Assessment is about the future and ensuring that the board's contribution to the organization is always top quality.

Exploring External Assessment

As an organization, how are you measuring and reporting success? Another unique factor in the nonprofit sector is how we measure success. In the for-profit world, many executives that serve on boards come with the mindset that the bottom line or how much was raised and spent is the barometer to measure success. That couldn't be farther from the truth and sometimes causes an emphasis on fundraising rather than providing quality programs with high impact. A board should use external assessment data related to program impact in the community to support marketing and funding strategies effectiveness.

Program Impact

To obtain this external data one valuable matrix recommended for the organization to utilize when developing a program and creating assessment strategies is the Logic Model developed by the Kellogg Foundation. The Logic Model is a format where the outcomes are determined prior to planning what is needed. Again, this is typically a staff role, but board members may have experience is some of these areas which can be helpful.

Marketing Strategies to Support Fundraising

Marketing and fundraising go hand in hand and should be viewed as a partnership especially if your organization is fortunate to have two different departments. However beware of standard branding strategies that emphasize an internal focus and branding. We are sure you've seen or heard marketing collateral where a nonprofit excitedly reports,

"We raised $100,000 last year" alluding to how many people support them. Effective nonprofit marketing for fundraising emphasizes the impact, uses empirical data and is designed to be donor focused. When creating effective fundraising campaigns or material it is important to use the external assessment data results to build a strong impactful story that is in line with what donors want to know. They will not be attracted to or compelled to donate to messages on how much was raised, nor do they want to support an organization that is struggling and this is their last ditch effort to stay alive. They want success stories using the data of how their dollars is valued and will have an immense impact.

INPUT	OUTPUTS		OUTCOMES - IMPACT		
INVESTMENT	WHAT WE DO	WHO WE SERVE	SHORT TERM LEARNING	MED-TERM ACTION	LONG TERM CHANGE
Staff	Workshops	Participants	AWARENESS	BEHAVIOR	SOCIAL
Volunteers	Meetings	Clients	KNOWLEDGE	PRACTICE	ECONOMIC
Money	Services	Agencies	ATTITUDES	DECISION-MAKING	CIVIC
Research	Products,	Decision-makers	SKILLS	POLICIES	ENVIRONMENTAL
Materials	Training	Customers	OPINIONS	SOCIAL ACTION	
Equipment	Counseling		ASPIRATIONS		
Technology			MOTIVATIONS		
Partners					

Another beneficial aspect of the fundraising and marketing relationship is the use of *cause marketing* by for-profit businesses. Cause marketing or cause-related marketing refers to a type of marketing involving the cooperative efforts of a for-profit and a nonprofit organization for mutual benefit. Breanna Schmidt of *Send It Rising Internet Marketing*, a leader in design and support of cause marketing efforts in the for-profit sector identified numerous essential benefits of cause marketing implementation. Summarized they include,

1. All parties mutually benefit with increased income and exposure.

2. Consumers have an appetite for social responsibility and cause marketing satisfies that need.
3. Businesses recognize that that it builds goodwill and their brand which will impact their bottom line.

To explore all the reason to pursue cause marketing visit:

http://senditrising.com/3-awesome-reasons-pursue-cause-marketing/

Fundraising

As with program assessment, fundraising assessment should include both formative and summative data. It is much easier to make corrections to fundraising programs if you are measuring leading indicators instead of waiting till the end of the fiscal year and relying only on trailing indicators.

Assessing fundraising results is an important function of the board. This is not finger-pointing or witch hunt to get rid of unproductive staff, but rather a sincere desire to improve performance. Often a full-blown development audit is called for. In this case, an outside consultant is called in to consider every aspect of the organization that affects fundraising (which is much more widespread than just—how much did we net at this event, or through this mailing, or how is our website donation program coming along.

Linda once had a client who said she needed a development audit but was afraid she wouldn't "pass." This is not the way to look at an audit, although we know that very word frightens a lot of people. But an audit can help you build on your strengths and overcome your weaknesses, to take advantage of opportunities, and to address threats up front.

There are many ways to evaluate your fundraising. Some are free, such as the Leaky Bucket Assessment for Effective Assessment (www.BristolStrategyGroup.com/nonprofit-leakybucket) and Special Event Analysis which follows. You may also opt for a full-blown development audit. Many consulting firms provide this service. Bristol Strategy Group also offers the *SMART Development*

Audit, designed in conjunction with Linda Lysakowski. Visit www.bristolstrategygroup.com/SMART-audit for more information."

Special Event Analysis

Events tend to be one of the leading fundraising strategies used by nonprofits. However, they often are the 'biggest losers'. For special events and similar activities, it is very useful to create a pre and post needs assessment such as the chart below.

This will help the planning process, measure outcomes, accuracy of the projections, and will help formulate the actual return on investment (ROI) data.

Event Name:			Date:		
Estimated Cost	$		Actual Cost	$	
Estimated Profit	$		Actual Profit	$	
Rank INPUT		Score			Score
STAFF HOURS Under 25= 5 pts, 25 - 100 = 3 pts, 100+= 1			VOL. HRS Under 100=5, 100-200=3, 200 + =1		
Rank Goal RESULTS High=5, Med=3, Low=1			**Rank # Results**		
Building Awareness			Taps Large Donors: 10+ =5, 5-9=3, 1-5=1		
Bonding Donors			New contacts: 200+ =5, 100-199=3, 0-99=1		
				GRAND TOTAL - Sum of all Scores	
Risk Factor Scorecard:					
24-30 pts: Great ROI, few things to tweak			**18 – 23 pts**: Tweak areas not getting the best ROI		
12- 17 pts: Recommended reworking of strategies/ problem areas			**0-11 pts**: Strategies need a major overhaul		

The Logic Model could also be used to help map outcomes. Measurements can be gathered from the following criteria.

Pre Assessment	Post Assessment
• Estimated cost/expenses • Estimated Income • Estimated profit • Staff hours required • Volunteer hours required • Risk factors • Sponsor/support potential	• New contacts acquired • Actual cost/expenses • Actual income/profit • Donor cultivation • Awareness/ marketing reach

Please keep in mind that this evaluation is subjective. For example, if an event is raising $1 million dollars but requires a lot of staff and volunteer time, it is probably worth keeping despite a lower rating.

BOARD BOUND LEADERSHIP *NOTES*

This is an image of the Action Plan.

To access a digital copy follow this link:

http://BBLeaders.com/action-plan

BOARD
BOUND
LEADERSHIP

Action Plan

ACTION
PLAN

Instructions

This action plan will help identify areas you want to improve, strengthen, or gain skills and knowledge to support being a great board member. By creating a personal action plan it will make you accountable to yourself and the organization you serve.

Initially only select three areas – more than that makes it feel overwhelming. As you complete a step – Celebrate. Then move on to the next step on the list. As areas are completed, add new ones to always remain in a cycle of continuous improvement and learning.

Category: [   ] Leadership   [   ] Governance   [   ] Assessment   [   ] Fundraising

Focus area Skills or knowledge desired	Strategy: Books, training, equipment	Target Date!!
1		
2		
3		

CHAPTER 8

Your fundraising will depend a lot on the life cycle of your organization (to be discussed in this chapter) but here is a good start to measure the different areas of fundraising.

Scoring point values: for each percentage award the equivalent point value. i.e. 100%= 10… 50%=5… 0%=0

Part 1 – Assess Giving	Score
Percentage of board making a meaningful financial commitment to the organization on an annual basis	
Percentage of the board has made a planned gift to the organization	
Percentage of the board contributed to capital campaign run by the organization (where applicable)	
Percentage of the board that attends events held by the organization	
Part 2 – Assessing Support	
Percentage of board that helps in developing long range and annual development (fundraising) plan	
Percentage of board involved in recruiting volunteer fundraisers	
Percentage of board that helps identify potential donors to the organization	
Percentage of board that plans and attends cultivation events regularly	
Percentage of board that has an adequate number of people with affluence and influence in the community	
Percentage of board that understands each member has a sphere of influence that can be helpful to the organization, and members are willing to promote the organization within their own sphere of influence	
SCORE	

Scorecard in the appendix

*F*undraising

Goal: To identify the boards role, best practices and strategies to create financial stability and sustainability.

The Future Depends on What You Do Today.

Ghandi

Ahhh, fundraising… It's a love/hate relationship and a necessary function in 99 percent of all nonprofit organizations. There are some nonprofits that are structured whereas fundraising is not included in the board's responsibilities, and there are those that are fortunate enough to have a dedicated staff to manage fundraising, however for the majority of grassroots, community based organizations fundraising is and will continue to be included in their responsibilities.

The reality is there is no need to fear it or feel as if you need to apologize when asking for support. With the right tools and some understanding of the numerous ways boards can support their organization financially, fundraising can become a system that is effectively accomplished year after year.

For the board of directors, fundraising encompasses several components that fall within the realm of both roles and responsibilities. But the problem is many board members fear the dreaded F word—fundraising! Why? They don't understand it, they're stuck in that "tin cup" mentality we discussed earlier, they aren't sure whose job it is, or they simply don't understand how to measure success in fundraising. So, we're going to give you a Fundraising 101 lesson and let you apply it to the nonprofits on whose boards you sit, currently and in the future. This is what will make you a valuable and sought-after board member. But first let's discuss an organization's Philanthropic Culture and the board's role in fundraising and why it matters!

Creating a Philanthropic Culture

To create a philanthropic culture, it is essential to first acknowledge that everyone associated with the organization should and can play a vital role in fundraising efforts. Too often the board takes on the assumption that all fundraising is the responsibility of the executive or development director as staff. They are only the hub of a much larger wheel and serve to coordinate unified efforts. Everyone in the organization should be made aware of their vital role as ambassadors of the organization or facilitators to identify and/or engage funding opportunities. That means everyone should be well versed on the organization's mission, program impact and goals, and needs of the organization (beyond monetary needs). They should be equipped with the tools to use their autonomy to engage in fundraising efforts.

> *ALL stakeholders should know and understand they have a role in fundraising.*

Here is a checklist that will help you assess the philanthropic culture of your nonprofit.

Answer with a YES or NO	Y	N
Does the organization have a Development Office?		
Do experienced professionals staff the Development Office?		
Does the development budget include money for professional development (membership in professional organizations, conferences and workshops, books and periodicals, etc. for the development staff?		
Has the organization allocated a budget for a donor software system to manage fundraising activities?		
Do the organization's staff members understand the importance of the development function? Do staff members support the development office's efforts?		
Does the organization seek to hire development professionals that are certified (CFRE or ACFRE, FAHP, etc.) or assist current staff in obtaining credentials?		
Does the Chief Development Officer attend board meetings?		
Is the board committed to development (do they give and get money for the organization)?		
Is there a Development Committee on the Board?		
Does a development officer staff this committee?		
Is there clerical support for the Chief Development Officer?		
Does the development staff act and look professional?		
Is the Development Office in a prominent location and does it have a professional appearance?		
Does the organization support the Donor Bill of Rights?		
Is the organization aware of and supportive of the AFP Code of Ethical Standards?		
Does the organization understand the importance of donor centered fundraising?		
Does the organization understand that it takes time to establish a development program, and that building relationships with donors is the key role of the development office?		
Is the organization committed to work with consultants when it is appropriate to do so, and not expect staff to manage major efforts such as a capital campaign?		
Is the CEO involved in fundraising?		
Are there volunteers involved in fundraising?		
Give your organization 5 points for each "Yes" answer!		

Scorecard

Results and recommendations

Score Value	
90 +	Excellent – your organization has an excellent philanthropic profile
70-89	Strengthen the areas that were less than 90% and make adjustments
50-69	The board needs help with its philanthropic profile; you might want to bring in a consultant to help raise your philanthropic profile.
0-49	Seek help right away to strengthen your philanthropic profile.

Why is Board Giving Important to Fundraising?

One of the responsibilities of the board of directors is to ensure the organization is financially stable however the implications of why individual board support is important are much larger than financial stability. The public wants to see that an organization's board supports and believes in the mission; and that board members are willing to make contributions for the cause. When an organization has 100 percent support from the board the credibility of not only the board but also the organization is impacted. Many funders will ask about, and some will require, 100 percent board giving before they will consider contributing.

There's a Right and Wrong way….
Make Your Pledge Now!

A colleague called Linda shortly after accepting a new development position. He sought advice about how to handle his organization's approach to board giving. He had just come from his first board meeting in his new position, and he said the board chair started the meeting by saying that board members were expected to contribute to the organization, handed out pledge cards, and said, "Fill out your pledge card and hand it to me before you leave the meeting tonight." Not exactly a well-planned, thoughtful approach to board giving!

Why Board Asking is Vital to Fundraising Efforts?

This should be no secret but boards play a vital role in fundraising efforts but it may not be for the reason you think. It is not about their ability to give but how they leverage their influence and speak up for the organization.

There is a direct correlation between the board's capacity to identify and connect with potential funding sources and success. Many board members express a fear of being "used" for their connections, however if you truly care (and of course, you should), more than anyone else, and committed to the cause it is a vital form of support. A board's involvement adds credibility to the organization and frankly funders expert it.

Now that your important role in fundraising has been clarified here are four focus areas that create an effective system to help you carry out the process.

Identifying: It is essential to recognize that being a board member is a proactive position as a representative of the organization. You should also dispel any beliefs that you are abusing your sphere of influence, rather using it to facilitate powerful community impact. It is essential to always have your radar on for potential funders, and, even if it too early to ask for support, add them to a prospect list to be utilized in the next step. Nonprofits that just expect their board to hand over names without knowing how those names will be used are making a huge mistake. Boards would be better off brainstorming about possible donors, sharing their insights and their willingness to contact these people.

Cultivating: This is the awareness or some call it the courtship phase of the process which introduces a prospect to the organization. This phase takes time and could include personally inviting them to an event, sharing success stories, speaking highly of the organizations, or simply inviting them to check it out. The organization can help facilitate this phase with tours, meet the CEO, host a cultivation event, or invite board members to participate in cultivation calls. Often many potential funders are lost because this process was skipped or the ask was made too soon. Cultivation events, such as a business leaders' breakfast, a cocktail party in a board member's home, or a lunch hosted by a board member at their country club, can be effective ways to build relationships, but everyone needs to understand that cultivation is *not* solicitation, it's about developing door relationships.

Soliciting: This is where the needs of donors are at the forefront, their interests must be understood and what it takes to attract them. Donors do not support need, they support success, therefore they should be approached from a peer to peer perspective coming from you the volunteer and the relationship you have with the donor. Know the prospective donor by doing research on their other levels of support and what types of causes they have supported in the past. This often will eliminate wasted energy on soliciting individuals or companies that have no interest in your cause. When making the ask, a team approach is best. But most important, start with questions like "What do you envision?" or "What are your interest?" The solicitation process has many facets and may take a while to perfect, but once the process is utilized the results can be amazing. One approach we both endorse is *Fundraising the SMART Way,* an orderly method for identifying and developing relationships with qualified fundraising candidates. This method provides aids for professional development personnel, and it also helps board members, volunteers and other staff members through the first two steps of the solicitation process, ensuring a positive experience. Because of the turnover of board membership, it is recommended to have ongoing training in these steps

Stewardship: The final step in the process is stewardship.. As we mention in the leadership module, a steward leader nurtures and develops human and organizational capacity. With donors, you've planted the seed now it must be nurtured which includes thanking the donors, recognizing the donors, proper use of funds, and proper reporting of donation. The board's role in these steps is critical. Thanking donors promptly and appropriately is important. It's about more than just sending them a receipt as required by the IRS. It means thanking *every* donor, thanking them promptly (within 24 hours is recommended), and letting them know how their money was used. It's also about appropriate recognition, based on board policies, and honoring donor's wishes to remain anonymous if they choose this option. It's about accurate reporting to the donor, the IRS (on your 990 form) and making sure the donors money was used the way they intended for it to be used.

Six Mistakes Nonprofits Make in Fundraising

1. Lackluster Social Media Presence

A solid social media presence is now a must-have for nonprofit organizations. Social media provides an additional opportunity for potential donors to connect with your organization and give to your cause. An active social media

> *You must learn from the mistakes of others. You can't possibly live long enough to make them all yourself.*
> *Sam Levenson*

presence is so powerful that *59 percent* of people who simply follow or like a nonprofit account feel inspired to donate money. With the potential to receive donations from over half your social media followers, there is more incentive than ever to maintain active social media profiles.

Despite the benefits, some nonprofit organizations cite time as a deterrent for participating in social media. But the risks of not having a social media presence can be detrimental. A lack of social media presence can:

- Be a missed opportunity to nurture supporters
- Eliminate a chance to secure additional support
- Upset donors looking to connect with you on these platforms
- Make your organization seem outdated

Nonprofit organizations who invest their time in social media have found it to be a worthwhile strategy. A recent study by *eMarketer* found that 71 percent of nonprofits agree social media is at least "somewhat useful" or "very useful." Additionally, social media is ranked as the second most important communication channel for nonprofits.

2. Not Diversifying Funding Streams

Probably the biggest mistakes many nonprofits make is not diversifying their fundraising streams. Many boards, if they're not familiar with all the revenue sources we'll cover below, fall into the trap of, "Fundraising is special events" or "Let's hire a grant writer; there's all this money out there from foundations just waiting to give it away." Just as business does better when it diversifies, so does a nonprofit. Imagine how many fast food restaurants would be successful if all they sold were hamburgers. They wouldn't be able to ask, "Would you like fries with that? or "Would you like to try our shake of the month?"

You should look at all of the strategies, and try as many as are feasible for your organization, based on your life cycle and given the resources at hand. Without other revenue streams, there is no way to safeguard your organization from uncertainty. In the section that follows is a details list of revenue opportunities that all organizations should explore to implement. Two great resource are the *Leaky Bucket* and *Fundraising the SMARTWAY* systems. More information is available in the appendix resource area.

3. Lack of Partnerships

Effective partnerships aren't created overnight. As with any type of relationship building, networking plays an essential role. Some organizations struggle to secure partnerships because they feel they lack the time, resources, and connections. Yet strong partnerships are worth the time and energy it takes to develop your network. A good partner increases:

- Your exposure
- Your chances of reaching new donors
- Trust in your organization
- Your credibility

Partnership relationships aren't only limited to corporations—they apply to nonprofit partners as well. Two nonprofit organizations can establish a strong partnership even if they have different missions: for example, Barbells for Boobs supports breast cancer detection while the Travis Manion Foundation supports fallen soldiers and survivors. Yet despite their different missions, they are able to partner to host and promote joint events. Partnerships are mutually beneficial because organizations are able to gain more exposure, reduce event expenses, and raise more funds at events.

4. Online Donation Platform Isn't User Friendly

Some nonprofit organizations miss the mark when it comes to website design. Many hesitate to spend the time and resources needed to wow donors in this department, but investing in tools like online donation platforms can quickly take your organization to new heights. With the right software, you can eliminate a lot of heavy lifting on the part of your staff and create pages in a manner of minutes that incorporate the elements needed for effective donor solicitation.

Some general guidelines, even if building your own platform, be sure your pages include:

- A bright, bold donation button at the top of your homepage
- A quick checkout process with as few fields to fill in as possible
- A simple payment processing system
- Beautiful images and branded design
- A field to enter a custom donation amount

1. Not Tailoring the Message

When speaking to your supporters, a one-size fits all approach just isn't effective. You need to understand what resonates best with your target audience. In today's marketing world, you will hear this referred to as your avatar. You first compile the unique attributes of your ideal audience and refine your messaging for the different segments within that audience to call them to action. *Fundraising the SMART Way* will teach you how to create and use your ideal donor profile.

Take this example into consideration: imagine you recently attended a fundraising event for a nonprofit organization. You had never given to this organization before and attended the event because a friend invited you along. You were interested in learning more about the organization's work, but then you received an email the very next day requesting that you join their recurring giving program. This hard ask might turn you off to the organization, as you don't feel informed enough to make a commitment. Had the organization chosen to share photos, videos, or a story about their work, instead of immediately hitting you with an ask, the messaging would have appeared more informed and appropriate.

> **The Story is Key**
> *At The Philantrepreneur Foundation we realize we can't compete with puppies. Certain nonprofits are like magnets and attract supporters merely because of the passion power of their mission — puppies, hunger, homeless and veterans. Your own story has to be passion packed and is so vital to long term success.*

Segmentation is crucial to ensure the right messages are sent to the right supporters at the right time. This can be accomplished by breaking your audience into smaller groups such as: first-time supporters, third-party supporters, and event attendees. Create content specific to each segment of your supporters to build stronger relationships. Stronger bonds with your organization can lead to a greater number of financial commitments from your donors.

6. Not Investing in Philanthropy

Many boards come from the perspective that their main responsibility regarding the budget is to keep expenses in line. But rather than focus on costs, they need to shift their focus to ROI—

Return on Investment. The old saying, "It takes money to make money," is true in the nonprofit world. Especially when the nonprofit is new, there are going to be startup, costs such as hiring staff, purchasing software, consulting cots, purchasing research services, and maybe even mailing lists.

Ongoing investment in the development office is critical—professional association membership and meeting expenses ongoing education, library of books and periodicals to help the professional stay on top of trends and new techniques in fundraising, and collateral materials are some things that must be invested in if your development team is going to be successful.

Funding Strategies and the Organizational Life Cycle

Many organizations don't realize there are numerous strategies available to generate funds. Unfortunately, only about 25 percent

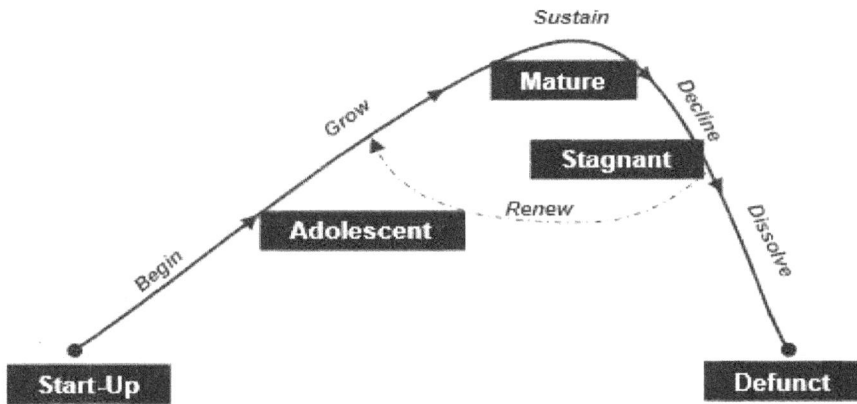

of the strategies are even used. This could be due to not being aware of them, not feeling the organization can do it, or not recognizing the potential of various strategies. You should also consider where your organization is in its life cycle and where the development office is in its maturity. An organization that is new to fundraising will be seeking more time building infrastructure, whereas a mature organization can focus on more cost-effective ways to do fundraising such as major gifts and planned giving. Below is a list of proven strategies that should be explored for your organization but keep all these factors in mind when deciding which are appropriate for your organization.

Memberships

One of the first strategies many organizations overlook utilizing is a membership program. First, to clarify, we are not referring to member-based organization such as professional associations, alliances, or coalitions. We are referencing the regular cause centered groups that need support. A membership program offers benefits that are easy to deliver, i.e. newsletters, member only events, and other mission-focused activities. A membership program can serve several important goals such as building mission awareness, steady income, increase your community outreach (database) and identify individuals that have an interest in your cause. It can be the foundation of initial fundraising efforts because of its simplicity. Staff members typically handle this type of fundraising and can be fully internet based for efficiency.

Donor Clubs

While membership programs are the first level of engagement, donor

clubs are the next step toward member retention and loyalty. Donor club levels are distinguished by levels of giving (gold, silver, platinum or understudy, director, sustaining) that provide an increasing amount of benefits and recognition. Recognition is important when initiating donor clubs and a solid plan for how it can be sustained. Individuals that have been nurtured through the levels of a donor club are good prospects for honor recognition and endowment consideration. Be careful choosing names for your donor clubs, they should be meaningful for your donors. A good example was an arboretum that chose donor clubs named after trees, with the tallest tree being the highest level—the Sequoia Society, and so on. A bad example was an arts group that named its donor clubs after artists and lost a big donor because she didn't like Picasso, the highest level, and chose rather to be a member of the Michelangelo Society which was significantly lower in size of contribution. Donor clubs are usually part of an annual appeal, a major gift program, and are also used in capital campaigns and planned giving programs.

Annual Appeals

Annual appeals are specific asks that have a designated time for the campaign and are conducted every year, such as *Mother's Day Appeal or Year-end Appeal.* A member appeal often is conducted near the end of the year focused on gaining new members or retaining current members. Program appeals can be for specific programs that the organization offers. It is important to note that language used in the appeal can dictate whether funds raised become restricted or unrestricted. Appeals can be done by email and telephone in addition to mail appeals. After the appeal campaign an evaluation should be conducted measuring success of response based on expenditures. Be aware that when you are acquiring new donors, i.e. mailing to a "cold" list, the response rate is typically 1 ½ percent. A solid response rate for renewing members is around 25-30 percent but the levels should be high enough to cover expenses and have a net profit. Phone appeals typically get a response rate of 30-35 percent. Phone appeals should only be done with current members or donors, and are a good way to renew and upgrade donors. Staff members generally organize and carry out these appeals.

Internet Methods

Fund development via the Internet is the fastest growing strategy to increase revenue. Approximately 64 percent of all donations are now through mobile devices or through a branded website. Therefore it is essential to setup a fundamental and solid internet campaign. E-blast, online merchandise sales, resources, and affiliations will all generate. A website can also speak eloquently about the mission and other important and unique aspects offered by the organization. These appeals are typically handled by staff; however, board members may be asked to use their social media networks to create awareness of the organization or certain appeals.

Special Events

Special events can serve several valuable purposes such as mission advancement, community service and fund development. When the initial plans are drafted, it is important to differentiate which of these is the primary goal to help determine realistic outcome and measurable benchmarks for success. Staff typically plan and implement events, but board members will often be asked to serve on committees or to run an event in a small nonprofit. Be careful that your organization does not get caught up in "special event fever" and runs too many events. Typically, one or two events a year are sufficient. Remember, events are not very cost effective

and can be a huge drain on staff, volunteers, and donors. Remember the special event analysis we gave you in chapter six.

Grants

Grant funding is specific in nature and requires the organization to demonstrate that funds requested will be used for clearly defined priorities of the grantor. Grant applications require a detailed *budget, program description, evaluation process,* and other specific information designated by the grantor. There are grants available for operational needs, but most are for a specific program, are restricted, and must be used only for the intended purpose. Grants are available through government agencies, private foundations, and corporate foundations. Grant proposal writing is a unique skill and often nonprofits will engage an outside consultant do handle this so its development staff can focus on other areas. Board members may be called upon to see if they have contacts with foundation officers that might be useful during the grant process.

Capital Campaign

A campaign specifically for funding that is designated for brick and mortar capital improvements. It has a launch with major announcements that detail monetary goals and the plans for its use.

These campaigns also utilized other strategies (grants, gifts-in-kind, named giving opportunities) to reach the goal. Most nonprofits engage a capital campaign consultant before they embark on a major effort such as this because it is a specialized area of fundraising. Board support of any capital campaign the nonprofit might launch is critical to success and board gifts will be the first ones solicited.

Planned Giving

The most common type of planned gift is a bequest which involves donors establishing or designating within a will or insurance policy that the organization is the beneficiary. Donor engagement and loyalty can be established via bequests and can be used in large and small organizations. A bequest as an insurance policy is a valuable and a viable strategy for donors because it emphasizes leaving a legacy and for a minimal monthly investment donors can plan for a significant donation. In the case of wills, a portion of the estate is donated to the organization.

Endowments

An endowment is a single funding account that is made up of numerous donors or from a single donor. It can contain gifts and bequests that are subject to a requirement that the principal be maintained intact and invested to create a source of income for an organization. Donors may set up an endowment to fund a specific interest; and/or a nonprofit's governing body may set up an endowment. In any case, an endowment requires that the principal remain intact in perpetuity, or for a defined period of time or until sufficient assets have been accumulated to achieve a designated purpose.

Bequests and other planned giving vehicles can also be used as they are received if there is an immediate need, or the donor has designated that the funds be used for a specific purpose that is immediate. Planned giving just like capital campaigns, the board is generally the first group to be asked to consider a planned gift when the organization is ready to start a planned gift program.

Sponsorships

A sponsorship is a relationship that can cover many different types of episodic or ongoing, non-philanthropic support. It is generally from the corporations' marketing department and this is where benefits to the corporation, *cause marketing*, weigh heavily into a good sponsor program. Sponsorships can be designed to support one event, a series of events, a special project, or involve a long-term partnership. Sponsorships are mutually beneficial relationships that involve the exchange of something of value from each participant to the other and involve clear responsibilities. Sponsorship does not strictly refer to cash, in many cases it includes a corporate donation of products and services needed to host an event, such as the venue, or produce a program or promotional materials. Sponsorship support is not considered philanthropic in nature because there is an exchange of goods (i.e. cash, promotional benefits, event tickets, etc.) and is essentially a contract agreement between two partners with specified *deliverables and responsibilities* assigned to each partner. To broaden the pool of potential sponsors, multiple levels and types of sponsorship are often developed to create opportunities for support at various financial or in-kind contribution levels. For example, a media sponsor typically offers publicity support, a sole/exclusive sponsor takes on the entire sponsorship responsibility, and a title sponsor is one whose name typically appears within the name of the event or product. The key is to have clearly defined responsibilities and benefits (for each level) and present them to a potential sponsor via

a written proposal. Like other activities that involve businesses, board members may also be called upon to utilize their contacts to obtain sponsorships.

Partnerships

Corporations are now favoring long term *partnerships* rather than sponsoring one-time special events and fundraisers. They look for strategic long term partnerships programs where they can get the best return on investment. For example, here in the Las Vegas area both Century Link and Nevada Energy will provide in-kind printing for organizations. It is an ongoing program that any nonprofit can take advantage of. Other examples include partnering with individual organizations to provide ongoing volunteers for program needs, or professional services such as marketing, accounting or other needed professional specializations. The corporations assign staff to support organizational needs. The impact of a partnership is that support is for not only your special events, but also your programs, advertising, etc. In proposals, every possible available benefit that they will receive for partnering with the nonprofit is detailed. Obviously the lower level the sponsorship, the less benefit a sponsor will receive. While staff usually negotiates the terms of a partnership arrangement, the board should approve these policies.

Passive Income: Affiliations/Services

Technology has made these strategies grow exponentially over the last few years. There are mobile apps, website links and numerous programs to select from. These services are

> *Passive income increases income without increasing workload.*

110

considered residual or passive income offered by an outside company that provides what is called an 'affiliate host link'. To start, the nonprofit organization connects with those companies that have nonprofit programs and sets up an account. Depending on the company it could be called an affiliate, partner, or even member but the purpose is to generate sales for the company and they reward you with a rebate/donation.

To be most effective your organization needs an interactive website to drive visitors to. This serves two purposes, increased awareness of your organization, and to take advantage of the affiliates' product which in turn becomes a donation link'.

When selecting a program, there are several things to consider such as time needed to generate support, and the rebate or donation percent level. Some of the largest companies out there make it easy to sign up but the rewards are very low. For example, a very well-known online shopping site that has a program for nonprofits offers back .005 percent which translates into $10,000 must be purchased for the organization to receive $50!! On the positive side, I guess that's $50 you didn't have before. In the appendix' resource area we will list some companies that offer nonprofit programs.

Earned Income

In today's environment, traditional fundraising strategies alone may not be sufficient for a nonprofit to grow. Even though the concept has been around for decades, many nonprofits do not seriously consider the possibility of generating revenue through earned-income ventures. It often is also called social enterprise and it can help:

• Generate new and unrestricted revenues

- Decrease reliance on traditional fundraising activities
- Differentiate themselves from their nonprofit peers
- Open new relationships with current and new investors
- Achieve greater mission effectiveness
- Serve more people better
- Attain greater long-term sustainability and growth

Earned income for nonprofit should developed and be aligned with the mission. The most commonly known are a museum gift shop or the thrift shop run by an agency like Goodwill. If earned income is generated from a totally unrelated venture, it possibly will be subjected to UBIT—Unrelated Business Income Tax. Regardless, many organizations feel this is worthwhile because it is typically predictable income.

The 80 Percent Club

Many nonprofits and board members think that most funding comes from corporations and foundations. Here is an eye-opening chart that every board member should be aware of: Recognizing that approximately 80 percent of an organization's funds come from individual donors yet, no matter if the nonprofit organization is small and large, sometimes they make similar mistakes across the industry that turn donors away rather than inspire them to give. Luckily, it's never too late to learn from mistakes and prevent future pitfalls. In addition to acknowledging your organization's own missteps, you can also learn from the experiences of others in your sector. After all, why walk down a path proven ineffective by another organization when you can take steps to be successful.

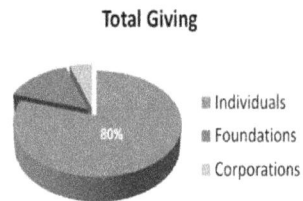

Total Giving

- Individuals
- Foundations
- Corporations

80%

This is an image of the Action Plan.

To access a digital copy follow this link:

http://BBLeaders.com/action-plan

BOARD
BOUND
LEADERSHIP

Action Plan

ACTION
PLAN

Instructions

This action plan will help identify areas you want to improve, strengthen, or gain skills and knowledge to support being a great board member. By creating a personal action plan it will make you accountable to yourself and the organization you serve.

Initially only select three areas – more than that makes it feel overwhelming. As you complete a step – Celebrate. Then move on to the next step on the list. As areas are completed, add new ones to always remain in a cycle of continuous improvement and learning.

Category: [   ] Leadership   [   ] Governance   [   ] Assessment   [   ] Fundraising

Focus area Skills or knowledge desired	Strategy: Books, training, equipment	Target Date!!
1		
2		
3		

CHAPTER 9

BOARD BOUND READY!!

Goal: Affirming your role as an effective and valuable member of a nonprofit board of directors.

Your First Step

Y After each chapter, we included a 'notes' page and at the end of each module a next steps action plan. We hope you took advantage of jotting down thoughts, focus points and those ever so important *aha* moments. Those notes should help prioritize to help map out your action plans.

ACTION
PLAN

We are not expecting you to accomplish or know everything at once but with every action plan there must be action! Get started and take those first steps to being a great board member. Make the process a part of ongoing development for you and your board.

With the Honor Comes Commitment

Board service is a privilege and honor. We know it brings with it some anxiety and fear but if you are prepared and knowledgeable about what to expect and what you need to do it can be one of the most rewarding experiences of your life. You have the ability to make an impact that could

> *We're not telling you it's going to be easy, we're telling you it's going to worth it!*

have long term results. You can change the world as a change-maker. It is up to you to meet the challenge of stewardship and accept the responsibility to nurture the organization and the individuals that will come behind you.

However, as you can probably guess we couldn't possibly include in this book every detail, situation, scenario or even the value of serving on a nonprofit board can offer. By identifying and detailing the Four Essentials of Leadership, Governance, Assessment, and Fundraising as the key elements we hope to start you on the right path to being an effective and valued board member – an asset to the organization.

There are also a few elements that fall within the parameters of being a nonprofit board member but not quite defined as a role or responsibility.

As a board member you must help the organization reach all corners of the community by becoming an influencer and connector within the community. If your

> *A comfort zone is a beautiful place, but **nothing** ever grows there.*

personal circle is limited to industry specific connections this is the time to attend networking events, and join local chambers of commerce and associations that bring together a cross section of individuals that may be potential candidates for board membership or supporters. Join industry related organizations that will extend your capacity but also keep you in tune with current sector trends. It is important to reach beyond your comfort zone.

With many years of work in the nonprofit sector we have encountered and experienced all types of situations and needs. We have taught separate and specialized classes on many phases of nonprofit management, fundraising and development, and we recognized there was a gap in learning opportunities for the individual board member. There was a need for a resource which would cover the basic elements to make your journey as a board member not only successful but satisfying as well.

Hopefully by reading this book you have acquired an understanding of your role. But it doesn't end here. With our strong belief in the concept of continuous improvement and learning it will help you face a sector and society at large that is forever changing. Even the unique nature of board structure involves a constant changing of membership. This means providing for that change is vital. With regularly scheduled training you can at least ensure your board is constantly equipped with the tools they need.

However, one factor that remains the key to success is the commitment and actions of a board. Therefore, we have created a **Call to Action** or our manifesto and we ask, as a board to accept these six action steps.

1. **Move to Impact:** Understand it is no longer enough to just "do good work." Nonprofits must create a theory of change and then find a way to measure and articulate the outcomes and impact they hope to achieve.

2. **Finance the Work:** Work towards completely integrating money into the mission the nonprofit is trying to achieve,

understanding that big plans are not enough, they also must finance them. And beyond just recognizing their lack of infrastructure, they put together a plan for raising capacity capital and convince donors to start investing in a stronger, more effective organization behind the work.

3. **Refuse to Play Nice:** Overcome the nonprofit norm of politeness at all costs and get real with funders, board members, or staff who are standing in the way of the mission and impact of the organization.

4. **Look Outside:** Understand that a nonprofit can no longer exist in a vacuum and that the board and staff must constantly monitor the external marketplace for changing client needs, demographic and economic trends, and funder interests in order make sure their nonprofit continues to create community value.

5. **Get Social:** Embrace the idea of a networked nonprofit and are willing and able to open the organization and let the world in as fully engaged partners in the work the nonprofit is doing.

Ask Hard Questions: Constantly force yourselves, and the high-performing team of staff, funders, and volunteers to ask hard questions in order to make sure they are pushing themselves harder, making the best use of resources and delivering more results.

NEXT STEPS

Board Bound Leadership: The Four Essentials provides the first step to becoming a confident and effective board member. Experience has taught us that, 1. we couldn't possibly put all the information in this publication, 2. opportunities to gain feedback, ask questions, and address specific needs is priceless, and 3. With ever changing trends and strategies, regular training is valuable. Therefore, our support doesn't end here with this book. Listed below are multiple ways to continue to gain the knowledge and skills for board participation, implement best practices, train supporters, and always have access to the latest trends. We also provided additional resources that are valuable or needed for organizational support and success. We are confident there are opportunities you could use now and in the future.

Board Bound Leadership can be your training partner because it is the perfect resource for anyone already on or contemplating serving on a nonprofit board. We can be your partner to help facilitate these processes for your organization.

Specifically for Nonprofits

✔ *Vet Potential Board Candidates*

We can help your organization vet potential board candidates. Ask them if they have taken *Board Bound Leadership* training. It is your assurance they possess the skills and knowledge they need.

✔ *New Member Orientation*

A long standing best practice for organizations includes providing new members with an orientation and board training. Let *Board Bound Leadership* be your go to resource. Provide each new board member with a copy of this book to ensure they get off on the right foot, understand their role and responsibilities, and become an asset to your organization right away.

✓ *Annual Board Training*

Every organization should conduct board training on a regular basis. Don't put another task on your 'to do' list let us train your board. This will ensure they receive the right information for your needs.

The **Board Bound Leadership** team can come to your organization with a tailored made presentation meeting your organization's specific needs.

Community Board Bound Leadership Training Opportunities

What's being said about Board Bound Leadership training.

"I have learned so much and feel better prepared to work with the foundation!"

"Perfect!"   "This is a must for everyone."

> *"I've been in the nonprofit sector a very long time and by far Board Bound training was the BEST I have ever attended in my entire career."*
> *Brenda Stout, CPA*
> *Las Vegas, Nevada*

> *"Who says learning can't be fun? Dr. Victoria Boyd and Linda Lysakowski, ACFRE present a jam-packed training into a series of easily understandable lessons. I still refer to the Board-Bound Leadership lesson notes and worksheets handed out in class. By the end of the day, I had the strategies to implement with my board so they can perform better together."*
> *Rob Cole, CEO*
> *ShoreShot Web Design*

✓ *Corporate Engagement*

Many corporation find great value in encouraging employees to engage with the community by serving on local nonprofit board of directors. Nonprofits love to have corporate representation on their board roster. Make sure your company representation brings value as an asset by understanding the unique role and responsibility of board membership.

✔ **Live Seminars**

Join us in Las Vegas as we present regular sessions in a small intimate setting. These training offer what couldn't be put in the book, personal attention, and your questions are addressed.

✔ **Online Training**

Check our websites for access to our online format.

To learn more about how we can help you or your organization, contact us today or visit our websites!
www.BBLeaders.com

Email:
Dr. Victoria Boyd: vb@bbleaders.com
Linda Lysakowski: ll@bbleaders.com

Additional Resources:
Dr. Victoria Boyd: www.Dr.VictoriaBoyd.com
Linda Lysakowski, ACFRE: www.LindaLysakowski.com
The Philantrepreneur Foundation:
www.PhilantrepreneurFoundation.org

APPENDIX

*T*he Unique For-Purpose Organization

Don't let fear guide your actions– understand the legal requirements.

Who doesn't fear the Internal Revenue Service? This fear often creates self-imposed limitations that are not based on fact. We have worked with numerous organizations that limit their own success and progress because they have misinterpreted laws or regulations, or arbitrarily set their own rules, thinking they were protecting the organization. It is vital that the leaders within the organization thoroughly understand what they can and cannot do. Many of the misconceptions are found in their understanding of the roles and responsibilities associated with being a board member.

Becoming a Nonprofit

There is an actual area on the IRS website (https://www.irs.gov/charities-non-profits/charitable-organizations/life-cycle-of-a-public-charity) referred to as the nonprofit life cycle which outlines the process to form a nonprofit entity step by step. It is a comprehensive guide based on IRS's involvement and timelines. However, what that process doesn't cover is the pre- planning that is so important.

As with every startup business it is highly recommended that a detailed business plan be developed. Its function is not to use just once, when you apply for your 501(c)(3) as some think, but rather to be a guide during the development process. It is a valuable process which helps assess if certain concepts or strategies are viable and often saves the founders post opening mistakes. Earlier we spoke about the value of the process journey and this is a prime example. We have our own life cycle process which we've discussed in the fundraising chapter because where you are in your organizational cycle impacts how you do fundraising.

This part of the process maps out essential elements unique to a nonprofit's needs. To demonstrate, here's a parallel comparison between for profit and a for-purpose business planning using terminology from both.

This chart is a very simplistic example of startup considerations. The main point is many nonprofits are started by some wonderfully passionate people that want to make the world a better place.

For Purpose	⟵⟶	For Profit
Cause or purpose	The problem	Customer's needs or desires
Program to fill this purpose	How the problem is being solved	Product or service to fill that want or need
Do people need our service?	Market feasibility	Will the customer buy our product or service?
Who serves this same cause?	Competition	Who else is selling this product or service?

However, they must discard the notion that the cause is enough. In the real world, it takes a well mapped out plan with strategic systems developed. One more example of the unique nonprofit – in the business plan they must develop two external marketing/branding strategies. One for those they support and one for those that they want to support them.

Ok, back to the legal stuff… but before moving forward a few words from our legal advisor.

State Level Requirements

What are your intentions? Within the United States of America each state determines its own procedures and requirements for nonprofit organizations. This makes the process quite complicated, however if you know your intentions, understand a few key elements and definitions it will help to clarify the process. The question is, do you need to file for full corporate status or just the solicitation requirement?

Corporate Filing

During the initial steps in forming an organization it must be registered as a nonprofit corporate entity in its home or *domestic* state. The organization's home state is its decision and generally determined by where it physically has a headquarters or office address, and where it delivers its programs and services. The need to register in additional states is determined by the scope of its services such as, will the organization deliver programs formally in additional states on a regular basis, which means will the organization initiate, plan and deliver programs, and seek clients and participants that are residents of that state. If yes, an organization needs to file a corporate application as a *foreign* entity. You already have a domestic status recognizing the original state as the *domestic* location.

The designation to note here are the words *on a regular basis*. Not having a state registration does not prevent organizations from providing services in a particular state. Often organizations are invited in by other organizations for occasional services. In this instance, especially applicable to organizations that offer portable training, workshop, or client support services, filing in that particular state is probably not required.

Regarding state taxes, each state requires nonprofits to register with the state taxation department to receive exemption from paying sales tax. For more information please consult a tax accountant familiar with that state's tax codes.

Charitable Appeal or Solicitation Filing

It is important to note that solicitation filing is a separate category from the corporate status filing. At the time of this publication there are about forty states that have solicitation filing requirements, yet all fifty have corporate filing regulations. Solicitation filing is one of the most commonly misunderstood and most often violated regulations. Even the states don't agree on or have the same definition and there is no set of rules that all the states use. The area with the most confusion is what constitutes ongoing and regular contributions and the definition of the word, *solicit*. The broad definition is any charitable organization that makes a charitable appeal in a state requiring registration must register in that state. There are some states that will provide a different answer depending on what department you are talking to.

The Charleston Principles, a document released in 2001 by the National Association of State Charity Officials (NASCO) came closest to outlining guidelines and called for a Unified Registration Statement (URS). However, even though it mapped out definitions and recommended guidelines it was not adopted by all the states so, although some states accept the Unified Registration Statement, there are still no existing or consistent standards that apply to all states.

The definition of the term *solicitation* itself should give you some insight into how to stay within the fuzzy parameters. Solicitation comes from the word, *solicit*, which means "to request." So, solicitation is the *act of requesting* and most people assume if you don't actively *ask* for a donation there has been no solicitation. These parameters are obvious in the case of email, direct mail appeal letters, phone calls, or other direct appeals. However, within the Charleston Principles they detail the definition of an interactive website which has a donate button as an *active* solicitation. Even if arriving at that site was for other purposes.

So, in an effort to try and set some outlines it relies on the definition of *on a regular basis* and *significant* portion this terminology was adopted:

To receive contributions from the state on a repeated and ongoing basis or a substantial basis means receiving contributions within the entity's fiscal year, or relevant portion of a fiscal year, that are of sufficient volume to establish the regular or significant (as opposed to rare, isolated, or insubstantial) nature of those contributions. States should set, and communicate to the regulated entities, numerical levels at which it will regard this criterion as satisfied. Such numerical levels should define "repeated and ongoing" in terms of a number of contributors and "substantial" in terms of a total dollar amount of contributions or percentage of total contributions received by or on behalf of the charity. Meeting any threshold would give rise to a registration requirement but would not limit an enforcement action for deceptive solicitations. For *example, a state might explain that an entity receives contributions on a repeated and ongoing basis if it receives at least one hundred online contributions at any time in a year and that it receives substantial contributions if it receives $25,000, or a stated percentage of its total contributions, in online contributions in a year.*

Federal Regulations

There are only four things the IRS requires.

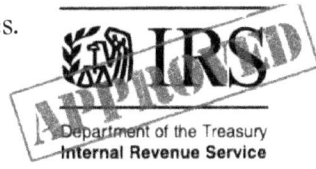

Taken directly from the IRS website this is the statement of eligibility where IRS identifies three criteria to get approval. To maintain eligibility a fourth requirement is an annual status report filing.

> *To be tax-exempt under section 501(c)(3) of the Internal Revenue Code, an organization must be organized and operated exclusively for (1) <u>exempt purposes</u> set forth in section 501(c)(3), and none of its (2) earnings may <u>inure to any private shareholder or individual</u>. In addition, it may not be an (3) action organization, i.e., it may not attempt to influence legislation as a substantial part of its activities and it may not participate in any campaign activity for or against political candidates.*

To meet and show proof that an organization is eligible to receive tax-exempt approval the IRS requires a governing document. The Articles of Incorporation and Bylaws are the governing documents for an organization and must be approved and signed by its officers. The IRS stipulates the exact language to be used for the (1) purpose statement and (2) dissolution clauses within the bylaws and then allows more variance in language for several other required items. The board of directors is responsible for the overall policy and direction of the organization and it is their responsibility to ensure that the bylaws are compliant. For additional policies, outside of governance, handbooks or guidelines can be created but they should not be included in the bylaws. Here's what IRS requires in the governing document.

1. The Purpose

Criteria one outlines why the organization qualifies for tax-exempt status and meets specific criteria. This statement must be included in the governing document.

> *Under section 501(c)(3) of the Internal Revenue Code and to received tax exempt status every organization must state be exclusively for charitable, religious, educational, and scientific purposes, or corresponding section of any future federal tax code and more particularly our purpose is to:* (this is the purpose statement of the organization from which its mission statement is usually derived)

2. Dissolution Statement

Criteria two which references prohibiting the earnings to inure individuals is met in several ways. The dissolution statement requires semi exact language stipulated by IRS. What is meant by that, an organization may identify another qualified nonprofit organization to receive their funding disbursement or leave it generic as stated below. The dissolution statement reads as follows:

> *Upon the dissolution of the organization, assets shall be distributed for one or more exempt purposes within the meaning of section 501(c)(3) of the Internal Revenue Code, or corresponding sections of any future federal tax code, or shall be distributed to the federal government, or to a state or local government, for a public purpose. Any such assets not disposed of shall be disposed of by the Court of Common Pleas of the county in which the principal office of the organization is then located, exclusively for such purposes or to such organization or organizations,*

as said Court shall determine, which are organized and operated exclusively for such purposes.

Additional clauses must be included to meet IRS regulations however some variance in language may be established by the organization and they address board member volunteer status, service, and conflict of interest satisfy IRS requirements.

- Board service policy
- Meeting policy
- Election policy
- Voting policy
- Conflict of Interest

3.   Public Disclosure

Even though the form 990 has been in existence since 1941, the **Sarbanes-Oxley** Act, known as SOX, which was passed by US Congress in 2002 adds additional protection for investors from the possibility of fraudulent accounting activities by corporations. The **SOX** Act mandated strict reforms to improve financial disclosures from corporations and prevent accounting fraud. Therefore, in June 2007, the IRS released a new Form 990 that requires significant disclosures on corporate governance and boards of directors. These new disclosures are required for all nonprofit filers for the 2009 tax year, with more significant reporting requirements for nonprofits with over $1 million in revenues or $2.5 million in assets.

Contrary to what some believe the Sarbanes-Oxley act was not implemented to create more control. Simply put it serves two valuable purposes, first it helps IRS keep track of what organizations are still active, and second it supports the public disclosure process. IRS had a database with millions of organizations that had received nonprofit status yet they had no way to verify if the nonprofits were still in existence. Following best practices that an organization should conduct a financial audit annually they piggy backed on that process to have organizations file the results of the audit. The 990 filings are then posted for public inspection.

QUIZ SCORECARDS
LEADERSHIP QUIZ:
ANSWERS:

Questions 1-10 are TRUE

Questions 11-20 are FALSE

ASSESSMENT QUIZ

Score Value	Results and recommendations
100 +	Excellent – keep the data flowing
80-99	Increase assessment in areas that resulted in less than 100%
50-79	More assessment strategies need to be implemented immediately. Seek training and support
0-49	Seek help right away.

GOVERNANCE & FUNDRAISING QUIZZES

Score Value	Results and recommendations
90 +	Excellent – keep the board commitment going
70-89	Strengthen the areas that were less than 90% and make adjustments
50-69	The board needs help understanding their role and responsibilities. It is advised to seek training and support
0-49	Seek help right away – your future is at risk.

RESOURCES

Best Practices
Guidestar.com
CharityNavigator.com
CouncilofNonprofits.org

Cause Marketing
Send It Raising Internet Marketing
www.SendItRising.com

Passive Fundraising Examples
Explore services your constituents use and need such as insurance and products, etc…
Legal Shield
Shop.com/Philantrepreneur
iGive.com
Amazonsmile.com
There are many to choose from.

Recommended Reading
There are many books in the marketplace addressing numerous topics related to the nonprofit sector. Board members and nonprofit professionals need to consistently learn new skills and hear new perspectives. Below is a list of books we recommend and many can be found on the Board Bound website (http://bbleaders.com).

Linda would like to offer a 15 percent discount on Charity Channel Press (www.charitychannel.com) or For the Genius (www.forthegenius.com) publications on their websites. Use the code **linda15** when ordering through their websites.

The Blue Sweater by Jacqueline Novogratz

The Networked Nonprofit by Beth Kanter, Allison Fine

The Five Dysfunctions of a Team by Patrick Lencioni

Charity Case: How the Nonprofit Community Can Stand Up For Itself and Really Change the World by Dan Pallotta

Forces for Good: The Six Practices of High-Impact Nonprofits by Leslie R. Crutchfield and Heather McLeod Grant

Made to Stick: Why Some Ideas Survive and Others Die by Chip Heath and Dan Heath

Seven Deadly Sayings of Nonprofit Leaders by Reid Zimmerman

The Leaky Bucket: What's Wrong With Your Fundraising, And How You Can Fix it by Ellen Bristol and Linda Lysakowski, ACFRE

Fundraising the SMART Way: Predictable, Consistent Income Growth for Your Charity by Ellen Bristol

Good to Great: Why Some Companies Make the Leap…and Others Don't by Jim Collins

Good To Great And The Social Sectors: A Monograph to Accompany Good to Great by Jim Collins

YOU and Your Nonprofit Board, edited by Terri Temkin, PhD

YOU and Your Nonprofit, edited by Linda Lysakowski, ACFRE by Norm Olshansky, CFRE

Give and Take by Adam Grant

Changing Minds by Howard Gardner

Difficult Conversations by Stone, Patton, and Heen

Made to Stick by Dan and Chip Heath

Start with Why by Simon Sinek

It's Your Ship by Mike Abrashoff

Getting Things Done by David Allen

How the Way We Talk Can Change the Way We Work by Kegan and Lahey